STONE AND MARBLE CARVING

STONE & MARBLE CARVING

A Manual for the Student Sculptor by

ALEC MILLER

With an Introduction by Lewis Mumford

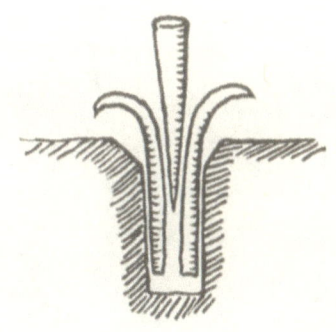

UNIVERSITY OF CALIFORNIA PRESS

BERKELEY AND LOS ANGELES

1948

UNIVERSITY OF CALIFORNIA PRESS
BERKELEY AND LOS ANGELES
CALIFORNIA

COPYRIGHT, 1948, BY
THE REGENTS OF THE UNIVERSITY OF CALIFORNIA

ENGLISH EDITION
COPYRIGHT IN GREAT BRITAIN BY
ALEC TIRANTI, LTD.

To the stonemasons of Oxford, England, who for more than a quarter of a century have helped me to appreciate the "mystery" of their craft: particularly to three—Harry Fathers, Tom Groves, and Tom Barrett, to the wisdom of whose hands I have so often been indebted.

Contents

Introduction, by Lewis Mumford ix

CHAPTER
1. About Stone Carving 1
2. Stones Used for Carving 19
3. Tools Used for Carving 29
4. An Inscription in Incised Roman Letters . . . 41
5. Elementary Work in Stone 51
6. Carving a Portrait in Relief in Limestone . . . 59
7. Carving a Child's Head in Marble 69
8. Carving a Draped Figure in Limestone 103
Index 119

LEWIS MUMFORD

Introduction

This is a book of craft and wisdom. The craft consists in the lore of the workshop, such as the master hands on to his apprentice: the nature of his materials, the tools of his trade, the detailed methods of work, the quality of workmanship. Wisdom, like art itself, is something else: the distillation of experience, transmissible only by example. Mr. Alec Miller has special qualifications in both departments, and therein lies the merit of this book.

That distinguished orientalist, the late Ananda Coomaraswamy, used to insist that art could be properly understood only in its original Greek sense, as technics, and that the artist was more akin to the engineer than to either the poet or the saint, though as the servant of the human imagination he might translate the intuitions of philosophy or religion into visible forms of wood, clay, or stone. At all events it is this elemental substratum of all art, the use of tools for the transformation of suitable materials, that Mr. Alec Miller treats of, or rather demonstrates, in the present book. Doing so, he passes on to the beginner the practice and skill of a lifetime.

Alec Miller belongs to the generation of English craftsmen and artists who, under the intellectual leadership of John Ruskin and the workmanlike example of William Morris, renewed the eroded and defaced traditions of craftsmanship. While few in numbers, these men were a mighty band: they included De Morgan in ceramics, Ernest Gimson in furniture making, W. R. Lethaby and C. R. Ashbee in architecture; and though their movement in its origin seemed a mere return to *medievalism, it turned out, in the second generation, to have a more positive basis: in the act of renewing a lapsed tradition, they made new forms possible, indeed inevitable.*

The gentlemanly precedents of the Renaissance had established a barrier between esthetic intuition and execution: craftsmanship became progressively the practice of menials and drudges, and by the middle of the nineteenth century had reached its nadir. One remembers that when Woodward, the architect of the Natural-History Museum at Oxford needed skilled stone carvers working directly, to carve the capitals on the columns, it was necessary to import competent workmen from Dublin. This weakness was particularly noticeable in sculpture; for the practice of carving directly in wood or stone had given way to the less exacting technique of working in clay. Indeed, in our own generation one sculptor still in her thirties has told me that it was impossible for an American student to find in Paris a studio where direct carving was taught and practiced.

Now honest clay modeling of course has it place among the major arts; we perhaps forget too easily that the stone sculptures of Greece were accompanied by magnificent bronzes, because those bronzes were later melted down to serve baser purposes. But if the ultimate product of the sculptor is to be translated into stone, that product had better be hewn by the sculptor himself, and not by any merely manual copyist—if only because, as Mr. Miller points out in regard to copies of Rodin's statues, the points left by the copyist's pointing tool may remain on the statue, to disclose to knowing eyes that it did not come directly from the master's hand.

The material and the process of carving, furthermore, control and direct the sculptor's imagination; indeed, one psychologist has even suggested that the technical medium exercises a sort of hypnosis, which brings to the level of the conscious mind the deeper feelings of the artist. Michelangelo

INTRODUCTION xi

could never look at a block of stone, it would seem, without conceiving the figure that he might reveal in it, already potential in the very dimensions of the stone. And the fact that a sculptor's mistakes, when he works in stone, are always dangerous, and sometimes irretrievable, gives the whole job a special kind of moral discipline, demanding foresight, prudence, wariness, and willingness to face heavy risks.

Mr. Miller comes from Scotland, a land whose masonry buildings carry on the elemental traditions of the stone carver. Born in 1879, he himself was apprenticed to a wood carver in Glasgow at the age of 13; and ten years later, when his apprenticeship was served, he went to England to join the Guild of Handicraft which Ashbee had brought together in the town of Chipping-Campden in the Cotswolds: a little town that itself is one of the finest monuments of late medieval art. His own works in architectural sculpture range from Coventry Cathedral, where he did a figure of St. Michael in teakwood, to Bryn Mawr College, where he wrought a series of gargoyles some thirty years ago. That combination of a thorough apprenticeship and a wide range of practical experience, making a special image for a special setting, renewed the ancient and deeply healthy tradition of the artist as master craftsman. So in this simple, lucid manual of workshop practice lies the funded knowledge of more than forty years of work.

We in America have been fortunate in having in our midst this artist and craftsman who belongs, as it were, to the apostolic succession which can be traced back through Morris and Ruskin. The foundation these men laid is a solid one, embedded in a deep respect for the tool and the hand that holds it, for the material and the mind that seeks to shape it. As for the tradition they have renewed, it is not a fashion in art, but a principle of life, and the root of that principle is workmanlike competence and integrity. If this manual taught nothing else, that lesson would be precious beyond words.

CHAPTER 1

About Stone Carving

This book does not profess to teach a reader *the* way to carve stone, but only *a* way. It describes technical methods which I have developed and used over a period of about forty years. Necessarily, in the early stages of my experience in stone carving I had to learn much by experiment, much also by mistakes; and it was only gradually that the technique herein described was worked out in such detail as to include the progression from simple relief carving, such as one might find on old tombstones, to the carving of portraiture, and of nude and draped figures designed for the garden or for ecclesiastical sculpture. Other sculptors (or carvers), no doubt, use other methods, and perhaps with better results; but I can describe in detail only such methods as I have consistently practiced, and I have tried in this book to make a distinction between difficulties due to inexperience and the other difficulties inherent in the practice of any art.

There is no easy way in which a technique of carving, or any other art, can be readily acquired; and reading this book, or any other book, will not of itself give a student the sense of form or the creative urge necessary to conceive a work of art and then to translate it into stone. I hope, however, that the book may be of use in suggesting methods and technical devices which will help a student to realize in stone the concepts of the mind; concepts which may be arrived at by many methods: by copying or derivation from other sculptures, by study and contemplation, by drawing or modeling preliminary studies, or by a combination of all these. The essential point is to have as clear a concept as possible before putting a chisel to the stone.

The word "carver" is today often used as meaning a person who copies in stone or marble a form or model made by another person, the so-called "sculptor." This is a misuse of the word, and throughout this book I use the word "carving" as implying generally a creative process and not merely a reproductive one. Mine is not a new use of the word, but rather a return to old usage. Recent writers on sculpture have had much to say about sculpture *en taille directe,* and many seem to think that this is a new method of work; actually it is the oldest of all sculptural processes and was constantly practiced from primitive times to the Renaissance. The myriads of stone figures, beasts, and decorative details of foliage which adorn the churches and cathedrals of northern Europe were carved directly in stone by men who never saw or thought of clay models as preliminary to their work and whose whole practice was based on an acquired technique which may have begun with simple masonry and only gradually reached the more complicated forms of animals, foliage, and figures. Their schools were masons' yards. They worked in a living tradition of architecture, and best of all, they had continuous work. Direct carving is ancient and long established, but it should be emphasized that there is nothing primitive about it. Because certain well-known carvers like Eric Gill have worked in a rather hieratic and archaic style, some critics and writers on sculpture seem to assume that archaism and simple contours are implicit in the process of direct carving. Nothing could be more untrue, as is shown in the numberless statues produced during the four centuries of medieval art. The methods and tools which I describe are such as I believe were used by those medieval carvers, who are variously described in contemporary records as "mason," "carver," "kerver," "imager," "imaginator." Given a block of stone and, say, two dozen chisels and a hammer (and the tools of today are very similar to those of the medieval mason-carver), the methods of removing the surplus material must always be much the same. It is true that today there are more elaborate measuring devices than were known before, and there is also available today power to operate electrical or pneumatic drills and chisels, which may be used if accessible and if it is found that their use makes work easier or quicker (by no means always the case); but I believe the best way to make a stone statue is to follow methods as near as possible to those of the carvers whose work still moves us at Chartres, Rheims, Lincoln, or Westminster, for in spite of all our mechanism, we cannot improve on these methods, and we have not yet produced better sculpture. In the following chapters, for examples of materials and technical methods, I have taken my illustrations from carvings from ancient Egypt, Greece, and the European Middle Ages, epochs in which the technique of carving reached a high standard. The practice of stone carving began when primitive man flaked flints with a bone or stone hammer, or shaped stone by bruising it with a harder stone. After metals were discovered, it was some time before they were put into use, as each in turn was at first exceedingly precious. Neither the finding of bronze (*ca.* 2000 B.C.) nor the later discovery of iron at about the time of the Assyrian Empire (ninth to seventh centuries B.C.) affected the craft of sculptor and mason at once. Bronze tools did not immediately supplant those of stone, and chisels, points, and other tools of bronze were probably in use long after iron was known, but it was undoubtedly the discovery of metals that gave the first great impetus to the craft. Egypt offers the best, as well as probably the earliest, examples of stone carving in historic times. The sculptors of Egypt as early as the Old Kingdom (*ca.* 3000 B.C.) used for their sculptures every available stone: red sandstone, white limestone, all the igneous stones, granite, syenite, diorite, basalt; and it is to Egypt that one must turn for the best and noblest examples of stone sculpture. The great Sphinx cut in

Photo copyright by Lindley F. Hall.

Fig. 1. The Sphinx, carved from an outcrop of red sandstone.

the living sandstone on a gigantic scale could not have been carved except by workmen with a long tradition of skill in their craft and aided by knowledge of something like our modern science of mathematical measurement and propor-

ABOUT STONE CARVING

tion. A recent work comparable in scale is the group of four presidents carved in the marble mountains of South Dakota. To create this, Gutzon Borglum made use of every available

Photo by Ewing Galloway.

Fig. 2. Mount Rushmore National Memorial, carved from the marble mountains of South Dakota.

device that modern science has produced: projection by photography, blasting with dynamite and other explosives, electrical drilling and tooling, none of which were known to the Egyptian carvers; yet the fact remains that in majesty and dignity the Sphinx far outrivals the modern work. Egyptian sculpture was essentially a funerary art, and as such was under priestly control. The great statues of the Pharaohs were made to certain prescribed and fixed proportions which varied only in special circumstances, as under Akhenaton. This fixity of figure proportion gave a certain majestic and impersonal aloofness to their sculpture, although, as their religion held that the soul must be able to recognize its dwelling place, the heads were often rendered with a regard for exact and faithful portraiture. Still the whole sculpture had no disunity, because it was ennobled and controlled by splendor of style and profound, if instinctive, knowledge of material. This fixity of action and proportion is more apparent than real, for there are many divergencies; yet it does remain as a marked characteristic of Egyptian art. In this respect Egyptian carvings differed from Greek works, although Plato with his passion for regulation and authority commended the unchangeableness of Egyptian art.

The different qualities and characteristics of the materials used by Egyptian sculptors led to differing stylisms and separate schools; for sculptors trained in working sandstone and limestone would find it almost impossible to adjust their tools and their skill to carving granites and basalts. Granite, being hard and brittle, forces on the forms certain stylistic simplifications; undercutting and lightness are practically impossible. If today such treatment can in some degree be effected by means of electrically powered abrasive tools, those qualities are nevertheless inherently unsuitable to the medium—a fact which the Egyptians thoroughly understood. Indeed, no sculpture in the whole course of history is superior in its technique to that of the Egyptians. Yet their tools were probably very limited. They had some implements of copper and bronze, but chiefly their work was done by hammers and tools of hard stone. Their stone hammers must have been used much as the

ABOUT STONE CARVING

modern "Bouchard" hammer is used: the sculptor bruises the stone into powder on the surface, brushes off the dust, and goes on again. Abrasives were much used—emery, corundum, hard sand, grit, etc.,—and they had drills, including tubular drills set with diamond teeth. Contemporary paintings and relief carvings, illustrating masons at work in ancient Egypt, show the hard stone hammer (probably granite) for rough work, the chisel and mallet, the square, leveling rods, the plumbline—all tools still in use today. Egyptian bronze chisels are supposed to have been hardened by continuous hammering. Two such chisels of the Eighteenth and Twentieth Dynasties are in the Metropolitan Museum in New York, but whether these are tempered hard enough to carve limestone I do not know. They could not be used on granite or igneous stone.

If a student will study in any museum an example of Old or Middle Kingdom sculpture, particularly sculpture in hard stone, noting the technical skill of the carving, the refinements of contour and surface, the use of abrasives to achieve an exquisite finish, he will learn much and perhaps be humble before work of such beauty achieved with tools so few and so simple. Let him recall, too, that this elaborate and difficult art was practiced only in the service of religion, that Egyptian sculpture existed solely for the purpose of providing in the statue a recognizable and permanent dwelling place for the soul; then, perhaps, he will understand something of that strange and moving quietude which pervades all their sculpture. Let him compare this reverent work with the hard and formal work of Babylonia, the blood lust of Assyrian work, or with the quick and vital work of Greece; a receptive student will soon realize that sculpture is very literally petrified history, and that these works of long-forgotten men can and do reveal to us secrets of technique and characteristics of the artists, their age, and their country; that, in fact, "dead men" *do* tell tales—tales which can be of enthralling interest.

The tools and methods of the Greek sculptors, of the sixth and fifth centuries B.C., are the subject of an interesting and learned book by the late Mr. Stanley Casson,[1] of New College, Oxford. He traces the use of the point, claw tools, bullnosed chisels, small gouges, and drills, but he believes that the simple flat chisel was not in use until a later period. He shows interesting and convincing evidences of the use of slabs of emery or other abrasives. These appear to have been used much as metal rasps are used today.

A student examining early Greek statues—for instance, the Apollo illustrated in figure 3—may have noticed a curious squareness in the figure, especially in the trunk. It would seem that the sculptors drew the outline of the figure (keeping the Egyptian rigid medial line and left foot forward) on the front of the block, then drew the outline of the profile on the adjoining side, and proceeded to cut these shapes through until they intersected. The resultant rather square form was then rounded off a little, but often there remains this quadrature, this appearance of squareness. It was only with a developing sense of form and increasing skill that they achieved figures fully in the round—like the Apollo of Tenea, tense and rigid but full of life and giving promise of even greater things.

I have occasionally used the two-outline method of roughing in wooden statues by band sawing, and I have always found it dangerous, even though I took great care to allow an ample margin outside the actual line limiting the form. I think the difficulty arises because one draws, almost unconsciously, with some sense of perspective, and this distorts the actual shape. A simple example of this is seen in the shape of a short Greek chiton, or kilt, and much trouble would ensue if one cut to a line curved as in the drawings (fig. 4). Stone, of course, cannot be fret-cut, and the Greek carvers must have shaped

---

[1] Stanley Casson, *The Technique of Early Greek Sculpture* (Oxford: The Clarendon Press, 1933).

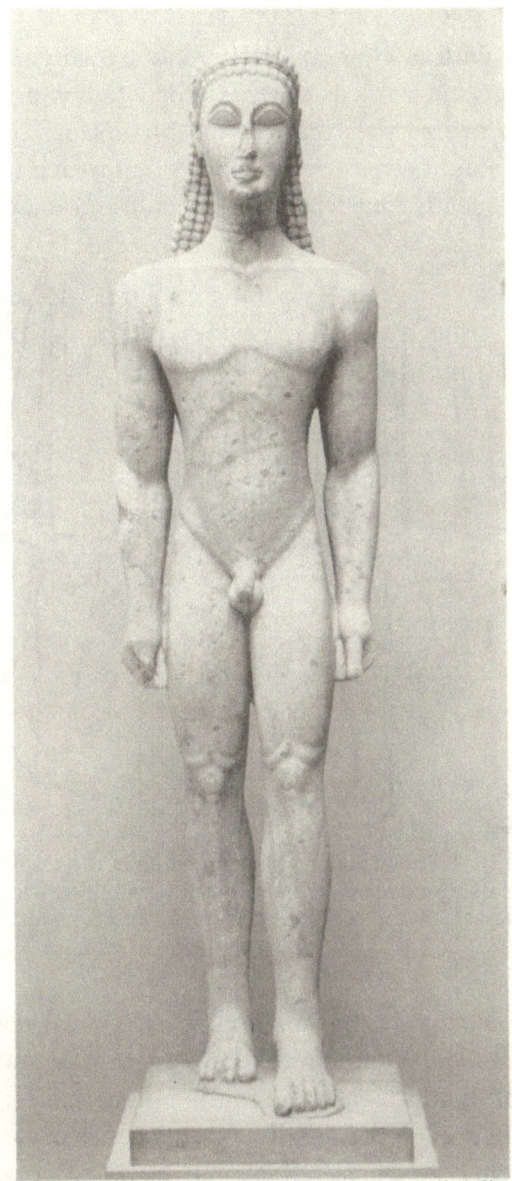

Courtesy of the Metropolitan Museum of Art, New York City.

Fig. 3. Archaic Greek Kouros, or Apollo, carved from marble near the end of the seventh century B.C. The quadrature of the trunk is clearly evident.

the forms with a stone ax or a point. I mention this detail because archaic work is much studied today, and students might not realize the cause of the quadrature or, realizing it, might think it a reasonable mode of approach to the form. My experience is that it is both difficult and dangerous.

Fig. 4. Greek chiton. The curved lines, the result of the perspective inherent in any drawing, cannot be followed by the sculptor; the true shape is a straight line.

Our knowledge of the methods of medieval masons and carvers is derived mainly from representations in stained glass windows of the thirteenth and fourteenth centuries, and from the small figures in the less important niches of many European churches showing craftsmen at work. So far as I know, there is no treatise on stone carving or sculpture corresponding to that on painting by the monk Theophilus,[2] which was

---

[2] Theophilus, *Theophili, Qui et Rugerus, Presbyteri et Monachi, Libri III de Diversis Artibus: seu, Diversarum Artium Schedula* (London: J. Murray, 1847).

ABOUT STONE CARVING

written about 1100, or the later treatise by Cennino Cennini,[3] which dates from the fifteenth century. Both of these deal fully with all the varied processes of painting and, therefore, have some bearing on sculpture, for all medieval figures were richly and elaborately painted. Cennini also describes various methods of casting in plaster. A sketchbook of a thirteenth-century French master mason, Villard de Honnecourt,[4] has survived, and has been published. It contains many interesting drawings of what he saw: figures, arches, and architectural details. There is a careful drawing of a dragonfly and an animal he calls a "lion," and there is an elaborate design for a perpetual motion machine, but although all the sketches are full of character and interest, they tell us nothing of the processes and methods of the carvers working around him. Perhaps this silence implies that such simple processes were hardly worth recording. These medieval craftsmen were too busy creating works of art to give much time to writing about them, and in some degree that is a regrettable loss. Many masons' tombstones are informative; some display the portrait of the mason with the tools of his craft—his mallet, square, chisels, measuring rod, and compasses. A craftsman's tools corresponded to a knight's sword or armorial device and were as proudly displayed.

There are probably people, even today, who think that all the imaginative beauty of conception and skill of construction in the great medieval churches was the work of monks, that the numberless statues were carved by brothers whose work on the scaffoldings was interrupted only for their orisons. This conception, of course, is far from the truth. These churches were the visible expression of the general will and beliefs of

---
[3] Cennino Cennini, *The Book of the Art of Cennino Cennini: A Contemporary Practical Treatise on Quattrocento Painting*. Trans. by Christiana J. Herringham (London: G. Allen, 1899).
[4] Villard de Honnecourt, *Facsimile of the Sketch-book of Wilars de Honecort, an Architect of the Thirteenth Century*. Trans. by Robert Willis (London: J. H. and J. Parker, 1859).

the community; the builders were animated by a very real sense of spiritual exaltation. Although it is possible that monks and other religious were the prime movers in the building and decoration of the eleventh- and twelfth-century churches, during the three following centuries many of the builders were lay workers directed by the clergy, who undoubtedly also decided upon the iconography of the decoration.

The lay workers were organized in guilds, which grew steadily in the Middle Ages. Under their jurisdiction large workshops arose, in which there developed certain characteristic schools of design with recognizable types of figures and draperies. It is not possible to understand medieval art or life until one recognizes that it was, in a very real sense, a communal and corporate life and that the buildings and art of the period are the expression of this group life, inspired by a common aim and working in a living tradition. The individual was merged into the community. That is not to say that there was no individuality in a Gothic cathedral. There are everywhere distinct traces of many individualities. One man's statues are influenced by some traces of classical forms, another's show that he indulged his fancy for the grotesque, and so on. Every worker had some opportunity for initiative, yet the whole building is harmonious because of the continuous living tradition of architecture and workmanship in which individualities are merged in the general unity. This dual quality, the single soul and the universal belief, is an essential characteristic of medieval art and architecture, and life. Similar work was being produced all over northern Europe; so coherent was the traditional style that it is often difficult to tell whether a work is English or French. Vestments or facial types carved by English workmen often closely resemble the same elements in the work of their French or Flemish contemporaries. Regional individuality, of course, existed. There are qualities in, say, the front of Wells, or in the Westminster or Lincoln angels,

Courtesy of the Metropolitan Museum of Art, New York City.

Fig. 5. The Virgin and Child (French: Île-de-France), carved from limestone in the fourteenth century. Shows original paint.

which have no counterparts elsewhere; but the similarities are greater than the diversities and make of Gothic sculpture a strangely homogeneous style.

In practice, as contemporary pictures show, the carvers of statues worked them on the banker as sculptors do today. Some work, of course, may have been done after the figure was in place, adjusting details or giving needed emphasis here and there. Since paper was virtually unknown in Europe until the fifteenth century and vellum must have been costly, much of this sculpture must have been done without elaborate drawings—perhaps with only slight sketches—and then set out on a whitewashed board as masons still do. Drawing is, of course, the basis of all sculpture, and no carving can be done without a feeling for the definition of form by some sort of line. Nevertheless, form in three dimensions is not just an extension of a two-dimensional drawing; a student has to learn to think naturally in terms of solids, and the way to acquire this power is to start with a study of simple forms, gradually working towards more and more complex ones.

The practice of drawing from memory was probably developed by the Greeks. The brilliantly skillful outlines of athletes in action which appear on Greek vases must have been drawn mainly from remembered observation. In France in the nineteenth century an elaborate system of memory drawing was taught by Lecoq de Boisbaudran;[5] and some artists—Degas, Rodin, and Fantin-Latour, for instance—owed much to this training. A part of this system was that students should always, after making a figure drawing in life class, make at home another similar drawing from memory. Camille Pissarro wrote to his son, urging this method: "You will have your difficulties, but a moment will come when you will be astonished at the ease with which you retain forms, and, curiously enough, the

---

[5] Horace Lecoq de Boisbaudran, *The Training of the Memory in Art and the Education of the Artist*. Trans. by L. D. Luard (London: Macmillan, 1911).

ABOUT STONE CARVING

observations you make from memory will have far more power and be much more original than those you owe to direct contact with nature." I would unhesitatingly corroborate that dictum and urge this method of study on all students of sculpture. I find in making notes and slight sketches for the carving of portraits, that in themselves the sketches may have value only as mnemonic signs, but the making of them helps to define the form in the mind, and the carving is done from this store of memorized observations. In working in this way one develops a sense of form and increases the power to remember and conceive (and memory and conception merge into each other) forms more subtle and of greater complexity. The power to visualize is capable of being extended and developed by practice, and direct carving is a constant exercise of this power and cumulatively leads to acquiring a quickened sense of form. The very finality of the process forces a student to define clearly in his mind the forms which he is seeking in the block of stone, whereas the practice of modeling, being a sketchy and experimental process susceptible of endless revision, leaves the power to visualize undeveloped and is apt to lead to the feeling of, "Let's see what it will look like this way." I cannot but feel that the practice of carving direct is a very potent means of developing the power of intellectual and visual conception which is so necessary to a sculptor.

It may be urged that direct carving is dangerous and likely to be costly in spoiling blocks of stone. This is partly true, but if a student wishes to make experimental models in the round, the easiest way is to cast a block of plaster to a simple scale—one-half or one-quarter full size (and remember that what is called one-half scale linear is really an eighth, and one-fourth scale linear is actually only a sixty-fourth, of the full size in cubic bulk). This block of plaster can readily be carved, and if too much is removed it is easy to add more—again, a thing not possible with stone. The advantage of a carved plaster model is that the approach is the same as that in carving the stone. The form is reached by the attrition of the waste material which surrounds it, and not, as in a modeled figure, by the addition of clay or wax to an almost linear wire armature. My own experience is that once a student or sculptor determines that the actual stone or marble sculpture shall be his own work and not produced by mechanisms guided by skilled carvers, sooner or later the models he makes in preparation will tend to become less and less complete and detailed; for every work of art requires a certain output of imaginative effort and he will find that if this is spent on the model, it will be indeed hard to keep up the interest and the creative urge in translating the model into stone. I am convinced that the total absence of carving in the usual training of a sculptor is a result of that wrong division into two processes, modeling and carving, and of the common acceptance of the idea that the translation of a model into stone is a mere mechanic's job, unworthy of an artist. One noticeable difference between carving direct and carving from a model is that it is much quicker to work from a mental image visually conceived than to copy from a model, not solely because of the time taken in measuring the points, although that always seems to me to be considerable, but also because of the fact that the existence of the model is hampering to free expression.

I am often asked, "What do you do if you make a mistake and remove too much?" This is a legitimate and pertinent question and there are several answers to it. Leonardo boldly says, "Those who make mistakes are not artists, only spoilers of marble," but obviously it would be absurd to suggest that one never cut too far, or never wished that it were possible to restore something which one had irrevocably cut away. But it must be remembered that the carver who is copying a model, either with or without a pointing machine, is in exactly the same position as the direct carver. He, too, may easily

ABOUT STONE CARVING

enough cut too far, or drill too deeply, for the machine is not wholly mechanical but is directed by human—and therefore fallible—will and skill. Let a student look closely at sculpture carved by highly skilled carvers working with every available mechanical pointing device, such as Rodin's marbles, and he will find that in every figure there are hundreds of small drill holes where the pointing drill has gone just a shade too far. Human judgment cannot be infallible, no matter how elaborate the guides, and mechanism may lead one astray as readily as the human eye. After all, it is the eye which finally judges the forms; and there is no absolute standard of right form, only relative right—each feature or detail is right only in relation to the rest of the work—and one must learn how to approach the forms gradually and without making too decisive incisions, which might make any modification difficult or impossible. I am certain that the dangers incident to direct carving are much exaggerated in the minds of many persons, and perhaps particularly in the minds of students and sculptors trained only in modeling. Again let it be emphasized that dependence on measurements copied from a model hampers the development of the power to realize a conceived form. Every student must work out for himself the relative amount of measurement required to achieve his end.

The august name of Michelangelo is often invoked, as if no one should dare to work in his method. He, it is true, did set a noble and, it would seem, almost unapproachable standard of excellence in sculpture, and he did this by carving either directly, or from what today would be considered small and inadequately detailed models; but it must not be forgotten that many hundreds of nameless medieval mason-carvers, for three centuries before Michelangelo, worked in exactly the same manner, and that their work shows deep feeling and consummate technical skill such as any sculptor today must recognize and might well envy. The art of stone sculpture will not again reach that height of artistic excellence until students and sculptors return to the simple integrity of technique of the medieval or the classical stonecutter. It is significant that Socrates, with his insistent and relentless passion for definition, was himself a sculptor, and the son of a sculptor. We may well seek in our work that quality of clarity and precision so marked in Socratic definition.

CHAPTER 2

Stones Used for Carving

In the course of sculptural history it is probable that carvings have been done in every existing stone from the softest chalk to the hardest granites and diorities, but I propose here to deal mainly with the stones most generally used, and particularly with those which are in constant use for decorative, architectural, and ecclesiastical sculpture.

Throughout England and America are hundreds of stones, most of them carvable. I have carved almost all the stones herein mentioned, and unless it is specifically stated to the contrary, the particulars given are from my own experience. (For stones available in the United States see the descriptive list on page 20.)

A student may be advised to begin carving on the softer stones. There are hazards to be overcome in each different kind of stone, but a stone that is not too resistant offers a better chance of achieving one's desired form than an intractable one; for with hard stones the actual process of cutting is both slower and more intricate, and though the student may have a clear concept of the desired form, he may find the realization of it too difficult. Carving a soft stone is only a little more difficult than carving plaster, and, beginning with simple forms, the technique of cutting is readily acquired.

The most commonly used stones are the oölitic limestones. These are found and quarried throughout the south and midlands of England and in many parts of the United States. Oölitic stones are formed of minute spherical shells which

Descriptive List of Stones for Carving

AMERICAN STONES

Limestones—Soft to medium hard.
1. Indiana Limestone—many varieties.
2. Utah Limestone—softer than Indiana.
3. Ohio Limestone.
4. Kentucky Limestone.
5. Batesville Limestone.

Colorado Alabaster—Soft—streaked with red.

Marbles—Hard.
1. Georgia Marble—many varieties of color and texture.
2. Tennessee Marble—some very white.
3. Vermont Marble—many colors.
4. Maryland Marble.
5. Pennsylvania Black Marble.
6. Colorado Marble.

Granites—Very hard.
1. California Granite—grey to black.
2. Dakota Granite—nearly white to dark.

Granites are found in many states but I have had practically no experience with any others than the above.

IMPORTED STONES

1. English Portland Limestone—very similar to Indiana.
2. English Bath Stones—several varieties—mostly soft and easy to carve.
3. Caen Stone (French Limestone)—cream-colored, soft and very easy to carve.
4. Pentelic Marble.
5. Parian Marble.
6. Sicilian Marble.
7. Carrara Marble.

resemble fish roe. In the many varieties of these stones, and even in different beds of the same stone, there is a good deal of variation in the size of these tiny particles and in the relative hardness of the stone. Shells, sometimes of considerable size, are found in nearly all oölites. If these occur in an important place, the best way is to chisel carefully around the shell (being very careful not to go below the outline of the final form), then to break it, or, if a hacksaw can be used, to saw through the shell. I mention this because I learned a lesson in dealing with shells in 1913. I had worked for three weeks or more on a garden statue of "Peter Pan" in Portland stone, a hard English limestone, and in shaping one foot (the figure was seated on a tree trunk carved from the same block) I came on a large shell in the ankle and used a little more force with the hammer on the chisel, with the frightening result that the foot dropped off. It is true that it was a big shell, and the foot was attached to the block only at the heel. However, nothing could be done but obtain another block of stone and begin again. The second time, I supported the foot by a tree branch. I had learned a costly lesson in enforced compactness of composition and the need for care in chiseling around shells.

All the oölites are, in general, soft and easily worked, but on occasion one may find them of the texture and hardness of marble. While such extreme variation is unusual, one has to be ready to adapt one's tools, technique, and time to great differences, and one must realize that the name of any stone does not imply a uniform standard of texture and hardness. Variations in hardness are sometimes disconcerting, and once a particular kind of stone has been found to be readily workable it is never safe to assume that another block of the same stone will be exactly similar in texture and hardness. Consistent evenness of texture is found only in artificial substances. Although the variations in stone are incalculable, it is necessary to assume, in practice, that all stones of the same kind will be reasonably uniform—and most of them are. Wherever possible, it will be safest to go to the quarry or stoneyard and test with a chisel any block from which it is intended to carve any large or important work.

Almost all stones are more easily worked when they are "green," i.e., freshly quarried. Most oölites harden and become brittle when long quarried. Stone then becomes more difficult to carve, and there is a greater tendency to "pluck"; that is, when a surface is being chiseled, a small piece, sometimes shelly, sometimes apparently evenly textured, may suddenly chip off under the chisel. This is likely to happen when one is finishing a surface and removing only a very thin skin of stone, and it is at this stage, of course, that plucking is most dangerous to the form. The only remedy is to be ever watchful, and to hold the chisel very firmly to the surface of the stone. This is more necessary in the final stages than in the earlier stages of the work. Soft stones are less likely to pluck than hard ones.

For general use in garden or architectural sculpture Portland stone and selected Indiana limestone are entirely satisfactory and, if seasoned carefully, may be used for outside sculpture, except for a figure actually standing in a pool—which should be placed on a base of concrete, hard gritstone, or even granite, up to or a little above the level of the water. Almost all stones acquire by weathering a callous surface and it is well to expose them to the weather gradually; if circumstances permit, a carving intended for outdoor display should be erected in spring or summer, and the callousing started before winter frosts begin. Any figure or decorative group in the round, if it is to be placed in the open air, should be "base-bedded," i.e., the strata of the deposit should be horizontal, or as nearly so as possible. This applies particularly to all oölitic limestones, and to most sandstones. If these are "face-bedded," i.e., with the strata upright, there is a danger that rain may soak down the softer strata and a frost then flake the stone.

STONES USED FOR CARVING

Nearly all stones, of whatever natural color, texture, or hardness, tend by weathering to become grayer and to lose their color. Always, any outside sculpture should be carefully weathered and gradually hardened. This is especially important in the eastern states and in the Midwest where there are great changes of temperature, and particularly where rain may be followed by hard frost. Where extreme cold occurs, garden sculpture may require to be wrapped in canvas and boarded up in winter. This is certainly necessary if the sculpture is delicate and has hollows in which rain or moisture may lie. The avoidance of such hollows is an essential problem in designing garden sculpture.

A very easy stone in which to begin carving is the fine limestone from Caen in Normandy. It is of a beautiful cream color, very fine in texture, and singularly free from variations of any kind, although occasionally large shells are found in it. It can be carved with wood-carving tools, and lends itself readily to high finish and delicacy of detail. It is much used for interior ecclesiastical sculpture in both England and America, and for this purpose, especially if the carving is on a smallish scale requiring precise detail, no finer stone exists. It can be had in large blocks, if large ones are wanted, and is almost the easiest of all stones to shape and finish.

One of the most useful of all carving stones is Indiana limestone. This stone is quarried in Indiana and is used throughout the United States for building and sculpture. It varies in texture; some of it is very smooth and looks almost like petrified clay, but on an average it is an excellent stone for all kinds of sculpture. It contains no grit and may be finished with steel rifflers or rasps, or given a high polish with emery paper. Few stones softer than marble can be polished, but this Indiana limestone can take quite a high degree of finish. Drills can readily be used on it and final shaping may even be done with carpenter's or wood-carving gouges, if care is taken that these are not ground too thin. For almost every carving purpose—architectural sculpture, garden or ecclesiastical figures, tombstones, or inscribed tablets for outside or inside use—this stone, if carefully selected, is a safe and good choice. There is a wide range of texture and hardness, and even considerable variation in color, but almost all of it is admirable carving stone. Similar limestones are found in Kentucky, Ohio, Utah, and other central states, varying somewhat in color, texture, and hardness. The softer stones should be used only for interior work or in the mild climate of the West and Southwest.

Sandstones, and what are called "gritstones," have usually a sizeable proportion of silica in them, and this complicates the carving because the silica acts as an abrasive and blunts the tools. Indeed, of certain gritstones it may almost be said that the stone cuts the chisel, rather than that the chisel cuts the stone. One of the difficulties in carving them is to find a means of tempering the tools so that they will cut the stone without blunting. Some carvers do this tempering themselves, but I have always found it best to have the tools drawn out and tempered by blacksmiths who are accustomed to their local stone. From my own experience in carving these gritstones, I should advise a student to provide himself with at least twice as many tools as for any oölite, in spite of which precaution he will find it necessary to have them retempered at least twice as often.

A very proper building practice is to use local stones for building and sculpture. Almost all stones wear and weather best in their own districts, and masons and blacksmiths acquire a technique appropriate to their own kind of stone, although it may be quite unsuitable to other varieties. A mason accustomed to softer stones is at a great disadvantage until he has readjusted his technique and his tools to the harder ones. A student called on to work in these hard gritstones would be well advised to spend some time in a local stone-

STONES USED FOR CARVING

mason's yard. Much is gained by this close association and, although the mason's yard has not the quiet of one's own workshop or studio, the compensations and advantages are very great. Almost all the sandstones are less likely to pluck if worked wet, and it is a good plan to keep continually soaking the stone. This also helps to keep down the silica dust and prevent it from getting into one's mouth and lungs (stonemasons who are constantly working these stones have a life span appreciably shorter than the average!).

No steel rasps, rifflers, or files can be used on any of the gritstones. The only abrasive which can be used for any of the varieties of hard sandstone is emery or carborundum. This can be had in blocks of various sizes and coarseness, and as these wear or are broken into smaller pieces, the pieces can be used much as rifflers are. Carborundum or emery should be used with water whenever possible, as otherwise the stone dust clogs the brick and it then loses some of its abrasive power.

It is inadvisable to attempt work in marble until one has had some real experience at carving stone. It must be understood that it takes much longer to cut marble than any of the freestones. The point used for marble should be heavier and more nearly a true point. The claw tools for marble should be fine-toothed, and it is to be remembered that the ratio between hammer blows and quantity of marble cut by the tool is much smaller than when one is carving the softer stones. The carving of marble is a process requiring patience and persistence, although it is not intrinsically a process different from that of carving freestone. All marble is crystalline and has no "bed" or lines of deposit. It may therefore be cut in any direction and, although it is hard and the pitcher breaks off much smaller pieces than when one is working in stone, yet with good claw tools it carves readily and is a singularly responsive and satisfying material.

The most commonly used marbles of antiquity were from Greece, and were either "Parian," from the Island of Paros, or "Pentelic," which was quarried (and I think still is) from Mount Pentelicus in Attica. Almost all Greek sculpture is in one of these two marbles, although some archaic work is of softer stone. Pentelic marble weathers to a slightly golden color. The whole of the Parthenon, including all the sculpture known as the Elgin Marbles, is made of it.

The great Italian marble, used since Roman times, is that quarried in the mountains around Carrara in northern Italy. Nearly all the work of Michelangelo is of this marble, and he spent much time superintending the quarrying of large blocks for the great tomb of Pope Julius. This, however, was never finished, the "Moses" (perhaps a symbolic portrait of Julius) and the so-called "Slaves" being the only fragments of that vast project which were completed. Since the time of Michelangelo, Carrara marble has been regarded as the finest for almost all purposes of sculpture. In the eighteenth century, Houdon, Canova, Thorwaldsen, Flaxman, Nollekens, all used it, and it was the favorite medium of the early nineteenth-century American sculptors—Powers, Palmer, Greenough, etc. It is still the marble almost invariably used today for portrait busts, figures, and especially for nude statues. Sometimes its whiteness is almost dazzling, and it looks rather like loaf sugar. There is another common Tuscan marble known as Sicilian, apparently so called because it all used to be shipped to the United States and England via that island. This Sicilian marble is faintly blue and has gray or blue veins. The impression it makes is one of coldness, and today it is used less than the whiter and more evenly textured Carrara, which remains the marble most favored by modern sculptors in almost all countries.

American marble suitable for carving is found in many states. Georgia, Tennessee, Maryland, Vermont, Pennsylvania,

STONES USED FOR CARVING

and Colorado all quarry marbles of almost every shade, from pure white to black, and of varying degrees of hardness. For sculpture, marble must be specially selected and it is advisable to see the block and test it with a chisel, rather than just to order it from a marble merchant. Each block should be tested for sound with a metal chisel. If there are flaws, sand holes, or fractures, it will not ring true. A little experience will enable one to detect the difference in sound. A flawed stone must be abandoned.

Somewhat akin to marble in appearance is alabaster. This is softer than marble, even softer than some limestone, and is very easily carved. It often has a transparent quality that gives it an elusive charm. There is beautiful alabaster in Colorado, streaked usually with red stains, but very readily workable, and for small and intimate statuettes not exposed to outside weather it is often appropriately used. Alabaster may be finished with good wood-carving tools. For the rough work finetoothed claw tools are best.

Granite is an even harder material than marble and, although it fractures readily and may be pitched with some freedom (using heavy pitchers and a very heavy 4- or 5-pound hammer), it is very slow work to chisel it. Today, with powerful abrasive saws, grinding wheels at the end of a flexible shaft, and drills, all driven by electricity, granite carving has changed appreciably, but these are not always available, and there is then no recourse but to the old tools, a heavy point, heavy chisels, and slow attrition with emery to finish the surface. The chisels must be thick and much more rigid than those used on any freestone, and tempered differently. A smith accustomed to tempering granite workers' tools will know the best temper for them, but freestone chisels, or even marble claw tools, are quite inadequate for working granite.

Another modern innovation is that of sandblasting granite and hard marbles. The method is to spread a thin layer of liquid rubber over the stone and then to cut the design, or lettering, through the rubber to the surface. The sandblast is then turned on and, strangely enough, the rubber resists the action of the sand while the granite gives way under it. In this way are produced in relief or intaglio almost all the tombstone inscriptions or designs throughout America. Of course this process cannot cut a perfectly sharp V for incised lettering or produce a quite vertical edge for raised letters, but with small coarse emery wheels, like large dental drills, the edges are easily sharpened and the incisions deepened. Electrical power and the sand blasting machine indeed threaten to destroy the tombstone maker's and letter cutter's craft altogether. A comparison between old tombstones, particularly those of England and of New England, with the standardized and mechanically produced tombstones of today shows how great is the decline.

Stones for carving weigh from 120 to 140 pounds per cubic foot. The approximate weight of a statue or carving may be calculated accordingly, although granite and igneous stones weigh more. A section of a tree stump, preferably hardwood, elm or ash, about 20 to 24 inches in diameter and about 2 feet 3 inches to 2 feet 6 inches high makes a solid and convenient bench on which to stand a stone block for carving; a stone for a figure not less than four feet high has sufficient weight to be carved without any fastening.

CHAPTER 3

Tools Used for Carving

Although this chapter deals mainly with the hand tools required for carving, it may be useful to glance at one or two mechanical tools or devices, commonly used today, which were unknown until the advent of electric power. The point at which a tool becomes a machine is indeterminate, but perhaps it may be conceded that where the modern power-driven devices are within the control of "the hand obedient to the brain" they are tools; where the power-driven device works independently of hand guidance it may be called a machine.

One of the most constantly used mechanical tools of today is the carborundum or emery saw. This is simply a disk of abrasive varying in size from about 18 inches to 3 or 4 feet in diameter, and usually about ½ or ¾ inch thick, mounted on a spindle and driven at a high speed by an electric motor. The stone to be sawed is laid on a movable bed, and as it travels against the revolving saw a powerful stream of water is directed into the cut. All the soft and medium stones can be cut quickly, the harder stones naturally taking longer. Care must be taken not to force the speed of movement of the stone. This method of cutting and dressing flat surfaces on stone has completely superseded the use of the hammer and the broad chisel known as a "bolster." The result is that today a stone surface is no longer chiseled ashlar or ax-faced, but is a mechanically smooth surface. Whether this sawn surface weathers as well as chiseled ashlar is doubtful. Many masons regard the bolster-cut ashlar as weathering better, and it is undoubtedly the more interesting surface; hence some architects get the mason to "run the bolster" over the surface, a device which merely disturbs a smooth surface by meaningless marks and deceives nobody; and others are even content to let a rolling machine make artificial toolmarks.

A very old, and still much used, form of saw is that known as the "grub saw." This has a longish steel blade, not toothed, but (as viewed edgewise) slightly corrugated. Either this is fitted into a heavily weighted wood frame, to be worked by

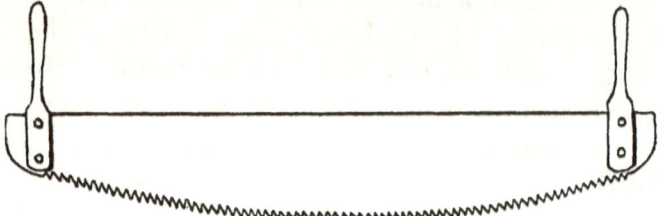

Fig. 6. Large two-handed saw, used for sawing soft stones.

two men, or it can be power-driven. The movement of the blade is back and forth, again a stream of water is directed down the blade, and, as it is working back and forth, there are ladled into the cut small sharp steel fragments called "shot," which act as quick abrasives. This is probably the oldest form of saw in use; sharp sand was the abrasive used, before the employment of steel shot. It is slower than the emery or carborundum saw, but very efficient, and not difficult to rig up if a power saw is not available. Soft stones like Bath stones, and softer oölites, can be sawed with a large-toothed saw, usually two-handed, about 5 to 6 feet long, and worked by two men.

I have already mentioned the modern electrical device of sandblasting for lettering and relief work. This, like the carborundum saw, is now commonly used and has almost destroyed the craft of the letter cutter. Other mechanical aids are those power-driven abrasive wheels, cones, points, and domes of emery which are fitted into a revolving tool held in the hand.

TOOLS USED FOR CARVING

As electric power is now available, these abrasive tools may be used readily at the end of a flexible shaft, particularly in finishing the surfaces and contours of hard and intractable stones, and in places difficult of access with chisels.

If the block of stone required for carving is of a simple rectangular shape, it is best to have it cut to approximate size by masons using one or another of the methods just described.

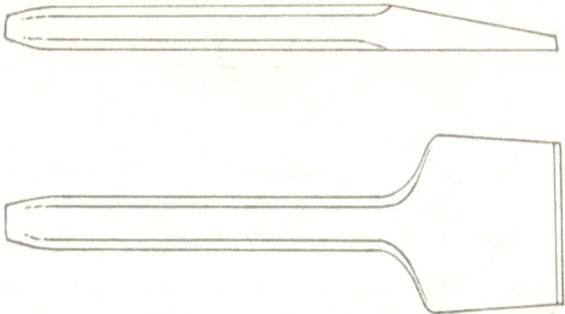

Fig. 7. A pitcher, used for rough shaping of the stone.

The size should be carefully calculated. Some allowance must be made for possible errors in carving, but if too much is allowed, one may find oneself doing entirely needless and heavy chiseling work by hand. I find in practice that for a figure about 4 feet high the actual measured width and depth on the drawing or model of the same scale might be 11 inches wide and 9 inches deep; but I add 1 inch each way and get the block 4 feet by 12 inches by 10 inches. (If the figure is small, allow something also at top and bottom for fixing. A 4-foot figure will stand by its own weight.) If the work is in a hard stone it is doubly important not to add too much, as the labor of cutting down to the final size may be great. On the other hand, if one gets the stone cut to the exact height, width, and depth of the model, then every decision concerning the disposition of parts must be absolutely accurate, and that is almost more than is humanly possible. Experience will be the guide. If the carving or statue is of a very irregular shape, the best way is to give the stoneyard masons two templates, front and side, in which the shape is reduced to its simplest contours, allowing a substantial margin. This irregular shaping is known as "scabbling" and is usually done roughly with a pitcher and a point. A pitcher is shown in the accompanying figure. It is a heavy tool with a broadly beveled edge. It does not *cut* the stone, but fractures it. The most useful size is about one inch wide.

Fig. 8. Blade edges of essential stonecutting tools. The deep gouge shown at lower left can be used only with soft stones.

The point is (I find in practice) not quite pointed, except for marble, but for any soft or medium stone it may be even ¼ inch wide. It should be of substantial thickness, yet not too heavy (unless it is for hard stone), and a convenient length is about 6 inches. It should be octagonal, and not less than ½ inch in diameter. For a simple relief carving, with perhaps some lettering, one should have at least 6 or 8 chisels, ranging in size from ¼ inch to about 1 inch in width; one large chisel 1½ to 2 inches wide for flat surfacing (often called a "bolster"), and several gouges of varied curves.

It should be noted that in carving stone a chisel may be used, working from side to side, to cut hollows such as in wood require deep gouges to cut. If a student has had some experience in wood carving, then that technique has to be laid aside. Stone tools being simpler, the carving technique is correspondingly simpler, and is essentially different. A light hammer is required—about 1½ to 1¾ pounds—and (or) a "dummy," which is used as a light mallet in finishing, where a greater delicacy of touch is required (for, unlike wood carving, practically nothing can be done with stone tools pushed by hand). A useful light dummy can be made by using a 2½-inch galvanized collar, such as plumbers use for joining lengths of pipe. A handle should be turned in hardwood, carefully fitted to fill the entire collar (though it need not be threaded, like the metal), and a further length of about 5½ inches allowed for the actual handle. Before fixing, make a saw cut about 1½ inches deep in the end of the handle which fits in the collar. This is to take a wedge, which should be sawed rather than split, since the sawn surface gives the glue a better grip. Spread the inside of the metal collar with red lead, "Cascamite," or other resinous or cellulose glue, and force the handle in. Then glue and hammer in the wedge. This makes a dummy of about 1¼ pounds and, if required, it can be further weighted by drilling holes in the end of the wood which is enclosed in the collar, widening these at the bottom, and filling with lead. Some masons always use a wooden mallet, usually of beechwood, but to get sufficient weight for heavy work a mallet is apt to be too bulky and a carver would do well to accustom himself to two or three hammers of various weights. For pitching, a hammer of about 2½ to 3 pounds is useful, except when one is doing work on a large scale and using heavy tools, when a hammer weighing about 4 pounds is better. On an average, I find that most work can be done with two hammers, one of 2½ pounds, one of 1¾ pounds, and a dummy of 1¼ to 1½ pounds.

The same dozen or fifteen tools, with the addition of some claw tools, will do for such work as the relief portrait in limestone discussed in chapter 6. The most convenient form of claw tool is that known as the "Scopas" claw-tool holder, into which loose claw blades can be inserted, so that when one edge of the blade is worn out it can be removed and reversed. These loose claw blades are made in sizes from ½ inch to 2 inches in width, and in two kinds of teeth, coarse and fine. (See fig. 10, *g* and *h*.) It will be noticed that the coarse teeth are ap-

34 STONE AND MARBLE CARVING

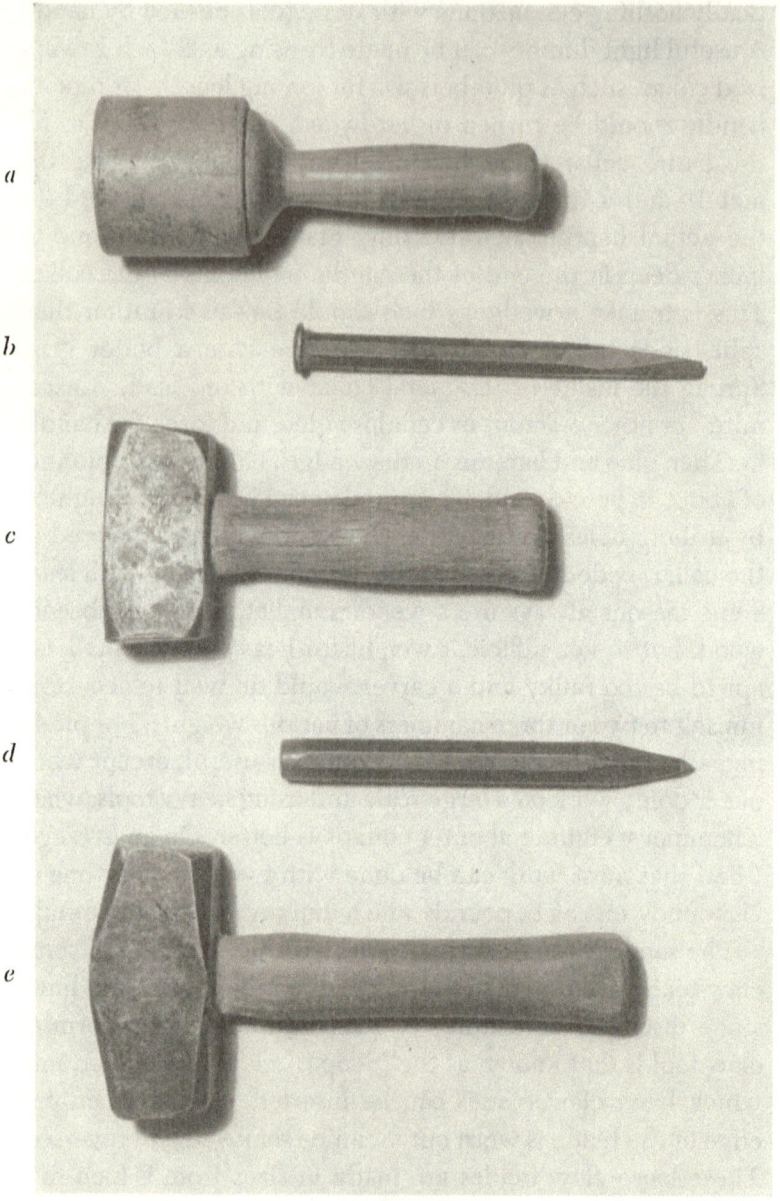

Fig. 9. Tools for stone carving (I). For detailed explanation see foot of facing page.

TOOLS USED FOR CARVING

proximately of the same width as the gap and that the fine teeth have a much wider gap. This proportion between tooth and gap changes as the blades wear down, for the tooth widens slightly. If the temper of the tool stays good, a claw tool is never better to use than when it is nearly worn out, if care is taken to sharpen it thin. Claw tools of smaller size and finer teeth can be made from small chisels. The best way is to get the chisel when it is freshly drawn out. Before tempering, the teeth can be cut either with a hack saw or with a saw file used at an acute angle. Then harden the tool to the proper temper; a deep straw color is usual. The temper required varies with different stones, and this is what a local blacksmith (or local mason) may be trusted to know. If the tool is too soft, the edge turns; if too hard, it frays and chips. Sometimes I have found, particularly with tools tempered for gritstone, that the first edge holds best. More often, especially with nongritty stones, the edge improves with use. Tools should be drawn out as thin as is consistent with keeping their edge and with rigidity in handling. No delicate work can be done with thick tools, even if quite sharp. It is not possible to have tools too sharp, though it is possible to have them so thin that the edge cannot be maintained. Masons ordinarily use a piece of gritstone and water to sharpen tools, but for many years I have found it easier to use a small emery wheel (5 inches in diameter) which, if used with care not to heat the tool, gives a finer edge and straighter bevel than is possible with an ordinary sharpening stone. For a finer edge, especially for working Hopton Wood stone or other hard stones, I use a carborundum

---

Fig. 9. *a*. A dummy, weighing about 1¼ pounds. *b*. Point, such as is useful for all the freestones, including Portland or Indiana Limestone. It is about 3/16 inch wide and is less stout than the one for marble. *c*. A small hammer of iron, weighing 1¾ pounds. This hammer, not being hardened, is less apt than the heavier one (*e*) to glance off the tool as one strikes it. *d*. Point, for marble; heavy. *e*. A lump hammer, weighing about 2½ pounds. This is cast steel and case-hardened.

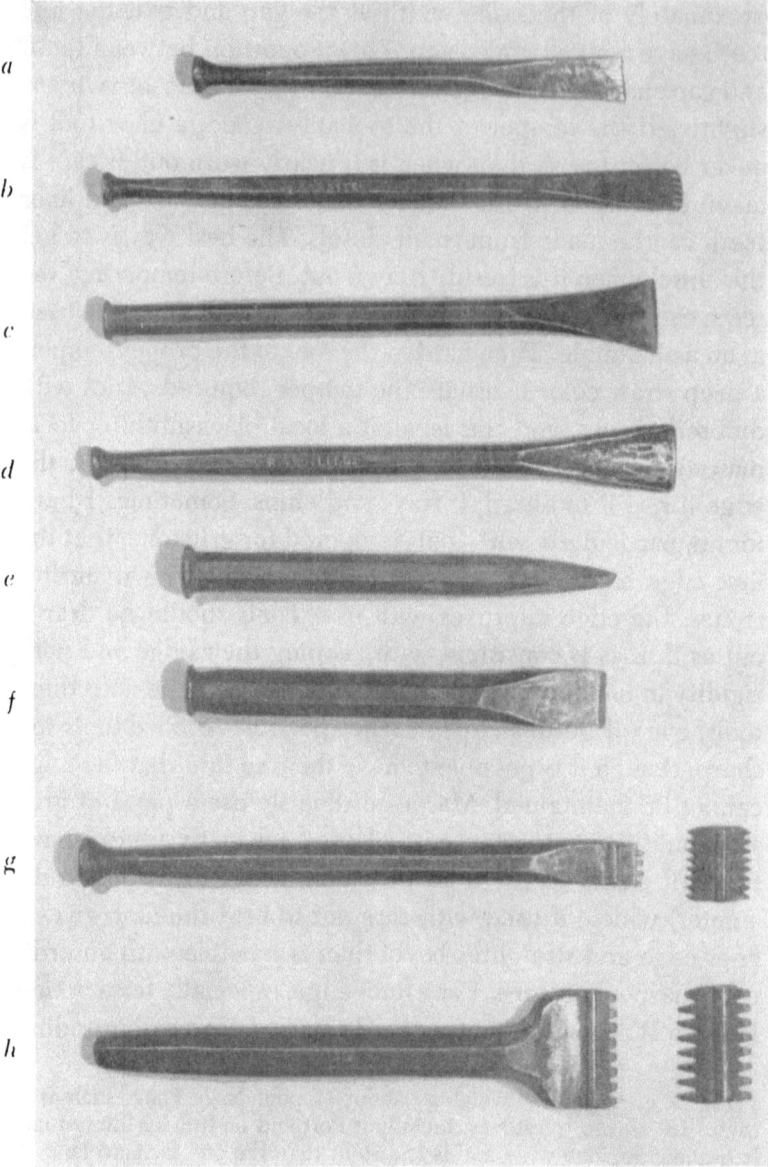

Fig. 10. Tools for stone carving (II). For detailed explanation see foot of facing page.

TOOLS USED FOR CARVING

stone after grinding and even, for final finishing, a strop as for wood-carving tools. A student must learn how to sharpen tools, and experience will guide him in getting the best use from them, for tools respond to individual treatment. Carvers usually use tools sharpened thinner than masons' tools.

There is a good deal of personal idiosyncracy about tools and their use, and a student will gradually find the angle of holding, the bevel of the edge, and the kind of hammer which best suit his own feeling. The aim is to achieve between the tool, the stone, and the hand a relationship in which the tool is so responsive that one becomes almost unconscious of it as one achieves the desired form. It is advisable to begin with a few tools, perhaps a dozen or so, and to discover by use all the possibilities of these, rather than to have many tools and not to know exactly what they are for. Tools are generally catalogued in two distinct groups, as mallet-headed and hammer-headed. Hammer-headed tools must not be used with a mallet (for it destroys the mallet!), although mallet-headed tools may quite well be used with a hammer, especially for finishing when the hammer blows are very light. The tools one uses for heavy work, points and roughing-out chisels, are apt to turn over at the heads after long and hard use. This gradually shortens them, but otherwise is no disadvantage.

Rasps, rifflers (which are shaped and curved rasps), files, (round and square), coarse and fine emery cloth (blue back),

---

Fig. 10. *a* and *b*. Fine-toothed chisels. One is slightly curved—"bull-nosed." This cuts a slight hollow, although it is not gouge-shaped in section. *c*. Flat chisel about 1 inch wide, drawn out to a spade shape. A tool for finishing delicate surfaces. *d*. Gouge about ¾ inch wide for use on any of the softer stones. *e* and *f*. Heavy flat chisel about ¾ inch wide. Sidewise view (*e*) shows thickness. This chisel is for rough work, not for finishing. *g*. Claw-tool handle with fine claw blade, used for marble. Blade is ½ inch wide. Loose blade, ¾ inch wide, shows the teeth unworn. *h*. Scopas claw-tool handle. The blade shown here is about half worn. The full length of teeth may be seen on the loose blade. Tool and blade are 1½ inches wide.

are all used in finishing the surfaces of stone carvings. All the oölitic and free stones may be so finished. It is worth repeating here: never use any rasp or riffler on a gritstone. Marble may be riffled, filed, and drilled. It may be highly finished with emery cloth of different degrees of coarseness. Certain hard stones, like Hopton Wood stone, can be riffled and filed, although the process is much slower than with soft stone. The edges of rifflers are sawlike, and the tool may be used as a saw

Fig. 11. Riffler.

in detailed work like separating fingers or where the use of a chisel is dangerous owing to the fragility of the carving. The use of rifflers minimizes the risk of breaking delicate parts. They are a very great convenience and their full use is found only by practice.

It is well for a student, in studying the sculpture of the past, to observe how the nature, hardness, grittiness, and intractability of different stones has modified the action or the stylism, and has forced on the sculptor certain conventions otherwise inexplicable.

Stone carving is dusty work and cannot be done in any room used for domestic living. The flooring of a workroom should be of concrete, or, if a wood floor is preferred, it must be on substantial joists so that no spring or movement is possible; and it is convenient to be on a ground floor, as heavy stones cannot be taken upstairs. A door wide enough to back a truck through is helpful. It is not necessary that a student should possess block tackle, unless he is handling stones larger than for life-sized figures. For large work I advise working in a mason's yard, where men and tackle are available.

Suitable clothes should be worn. A blouse or coverall of strong cotton or linen is essential; and rope-soled or light can-

TOOLS USED FOR CARVING 39

vas shoes are useful, as limestone dust destroys leather. A hat of some sort should be worn; otherwise the hair becomes filled with stone dust. I have for a long time used a wide Basque beret (not the little tight beret so common today). This large beret pulled forward over the eyes gives a good deal of protection from flying chips and dust; but any well-projecting cap will do. If one has to wear glasses (which are an added protection to the eyes), they are sure to get a little scratched with flying chips of stone. In any case, it is inevitable that some dust or chips will get into the eyes. Masons are commonly adept at removing these, using a looped horsehair, usually pulled from their banker brush—perhaps not very hygienic, but generally very effective.

List of Essential Tools

Rule and tape measure.
T-square, two set squares (or triangles).
Metal right-angle square, at least 18 inches long.
One pair of calipers opening to about 15 inches.
One pair of calipers opening to about 6 inches.
   (Proportional calipers are often useful. They should be large enough to open to about 18 inches at the wide end.)
Emery wheel, or block of gritstone.
One or two carborundum slips.
Rifflers 10, 12, and 15 inches long, curved at both ends.
One large coarse rasp, 12 inches long.
A dozen or 15 stone-carving tools. (These will suffice at first. Those illustrated on page 36 are the minimum. The smaller ones should be duplicated, and the number gradually increased.)
Two hammers, 2½ and 1¾ pounds. For large work a 4-pound hammer may be useful.
One dummy.
Hack saw, and blades not less than 12 inches long.
One crowbar, about 4 feet long.
   Note: Some carpenter's tools are useful for making boxes or devices to clamp work down and hold it steady.

CHAPTER 4

An Inscription in Incised Roman Letters

As lettering is constantly required on simple tombstones, or memorial tablets, a student should have some knowledge of the forms of good lettering and might well consult some of the best books on the subject. There is an exhaustive and well-illustrated book, *Writing and Illuminating*, by Edward Johnston,[1] and two recent books by Graily Hewitt[2] and Percy Smith,[3] which cover the whole field and are entirely admirable. A student would do well to possess and study one or more of these books.

Before trying to carve letters it is essential to know the characteristic forms of Roman capitals and lower case, Lombardic capitals, uncials, and minuscules, and Gothic capitals and script, as all these may be required. The inscription here illustrated (figs. 12 and 13) is in Roman capitals, perhaps the most generally used form of lettering. There are few or no rules which can be laid down for spacing inscriptions. Each text, or name, is a different problem in which the factors to be considered are stone, scale, spacing, position, legibility—all equally important. The spacing of letters harmoniously cannot be reduced to a definite formula of measurement; the aim

---

[1] Edward Johnston, *Writing & Illuminating, & Lettering* (London: J. Hogg, 1906; London: Pitman, 1932).

[2] Graily Hewitt, *Lettering for Students and Craftsmen* (Philadelphia: Lippincott, 1930).

[3] Percy John Delf Smith, *Lettering: A Handbook of Modern Alphabets* (London: A. & C. Black, 1936).

is to keep a relatively equal area between and within the letters, and this can only be done by eye and not at all by ruler.

There is one calculable measurement in incised Roman capitals; that, on an average, the width of the thick strokes

Fig. 12. *Line 1.* Cut with a one-inch chisel; gouges used for letter S. The bottom of the incisions is not yet fully cleaned. *Line 2.* The formation of the serifs. *Line 3.* Drawing only. *Line 4.* Carving completed.

should be about one-eighth to one-tenth the height of the letter; for example, in letters 1 inch high the thick stroke is about ⅛ inch to ⅒ inch wide. This scale applies to soft or medium stone and may be taken as applying to letters up to about 2 inches high. On larger letters, say 3 inches high, a width of ¼ inch would be ample, i.e, one-twelfth the height. In marble or hard stone a more graceful letter could be achieved at one-twelfth, or even narrower, but one has to remember

INCISED ROMAN LETTERS

that there is also a proportion to be observed between the thick strokes and the thin ones, and if one adopts a very slender thick stroke the thin ones may become too thin to be readily visible, or else there may be insufficient contrast between

Fig. 13. The finished inscription.

thick and thin. Usually, the thins are a little less than one-half the width of the thicks, and on large letters may be one-third or even less. In the present inscription the letters are 1⅜ inches high, and the thick strokes are about ⅛ inch wide, or about one-tenth the height. The space between each two lines of lettering can only be determined separately for each inscription, depending again on length, position, and legibility. In the example given here it is ¼ inch. If the inscription is at all complicated or long, it is well to set it out carefully on paper and then transfer it, line by line, to the stone. I say line by line, because if a long inscription is drawn on the stone it is very likely to get rubbed off as one works. A mason letter cutter usually works with the stone almost vertical and, to avoid this rubbing, begins at the lowest line.

My own practice is rather to work with the slab of stone horizontal or only at a writing-desk slope, on a bench about 3 feet to 3 feet 3 inches high, and if the inscription is at all complicated in spacing, to cut off each line as required from the

Fig. 14. The gradual deepening of the incision, following the method described in the text.

paper on which it is laid out, and then transfer it to the stone. A brief inscription like the example does not require setting out on paper. It was lightly sketched on the stone as shown in the third line, figure 12, page 42. The top line shows the first chisel cuts; one should cut from each side with a chisel ground thin and kept very sharp. It will be seen that the two cuts do not actually meet and that there is some unfree stone left in the angle. It is well not to try to get the incision to the full depth at once. The attempt to do so will almost certainly fracture the stone further than the width of the letter and so give it untidy edges. Care must also be taken that the edge of the letter does not break behind the chisel instead of only in front of it; therefore, tap lightly. (In soft stone use the 1¼-pound dummy.) Make a slight incision on each side; then go over it again and again, cutting gradually to the final sharp angle. In smallish letters, the angle is about 60 degrees; in large letters, it may well be nearer a right angle. The serifs may be cut either before or after the long strokes. The second line shows the serifs cut before the long strokes of the letter. To

INCISED ROMAN LETTERS 45

cut these serifs one requires a tool spread out to a spade shape; indeed, in soft stone it is easiest to use a curved spade-tool, i.e., a shallow gouge. Care should be taken that the ends of the serifs come to a delicate sharp point. This requires skill and very sharp tools. It presupposes also that the stone is susceptible of such precise cutting and that its surface is smooth enough for the cutting of fine lines. (I would suggest Caen stone or a fine limestone as suitable for a beginner at lettering.)

Fig. 15. The shape and section of the spade tool used for cutting serifs.

On large capitals, the serifs are sometimes slightly curved on the base line, which adds grace to them. It may be well also, with curved letters which touch the line of the height of letters only at one point, to make them a fraction taller, especially if they should come between letters with a long base or top line. If the main strokes of the letters are cut first, before the serifs, it is essential that the chisel should not be the full height of the letter. In the example given, with letters 1⅜ inches high, I used a chisel rather less than an inch wide; this allows for careful cutting of the serifs. Throughout the inscription it is to be remembered that all thin and thick strokes, whether in curved letters or straight, should be of similar width, and it may be necessary to cut the thin strokes to a deeper

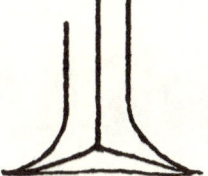

Fig. 16. The slight curve of the serif on the base line.

angle, perhaps as close as 45 degrees, to get sufficient shadow. Particular care should be taken to get neat intersection of strokes at the right angles in E, L, N, T, V, etc., and also where thick and thin strokes meet in an acute angle, etc., where great care is required to avoid a ragged angle.

Many letter cutters working in hard stone, such as Hopton Wood or marble, adopt an entirely different carving technique and, instead of using a wide chisel and cutting down to the apex of the angle as in this medium stone (see fig. 19, *a*) cut *along the side* of the angle with a narrow, thin, and very sharp chisel (fig. 19, *b*). This is a method much used by monument-

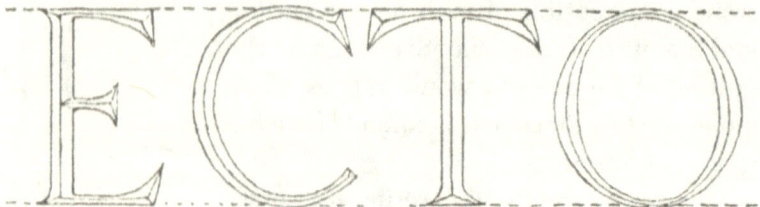

Fig. 17. Curved letters (here C and O) slightly exceeding the height of uncurved letters.

letter cutters and it can be and is used for curved as well as straight letters. It requires care in starting the incision and a steady hand and accurate eye to keep the curves graceful, especially where a thick stroke diminishes into a thin one, and

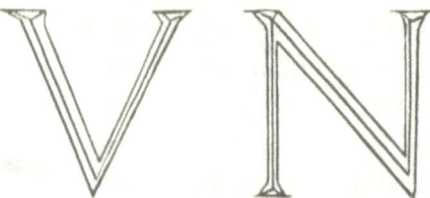

Fig. 18. Intersecting acute angles requiring special attention.

the straight incisions parallel and straight. Personally, I have seldom adopted this method, using it only when the letters were on a large scale that made the use of curved gouges difficult or impossible; but a student would do well to practice both methods of working. The late Eric Gill, whose skill in the technique of carving is unquestionable, used this monument cutters' technique, and the grace and distinction of his inscriptions cannot be surpassed. Of course a combination of

INCISED ROMAN LETTERS

both methods may often be convenient, and this lessens the number of gouges required and gives greater freedom in the curves. It should not be forgotten that the forms and contours of letters have a long ancestral history and were derived originally from pen work. Therefore, the thicks and thins may not be transposed or changed, nor should any attempt be made to achieve a quite specious originality by trying to invent vari-

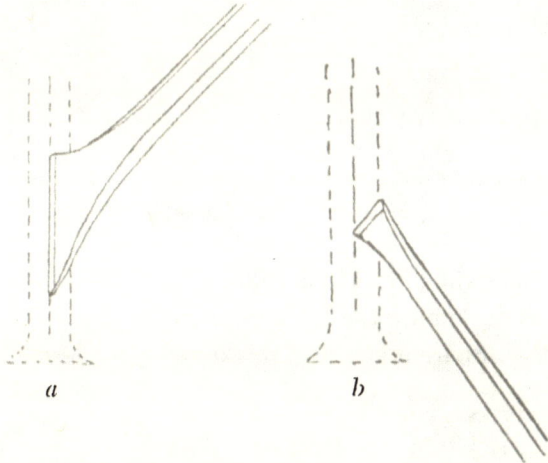

Fig. 19. *a*. Method of chiseling toward apex of incision: used on soft stones. *b*. Method of chiseling along side of incision: used on hard stones.

ants on the forms so developed. There is ample scope for skill in refinements of proportion and spacing and in the grace and beauty of the curves of letters. These, rather than any attempted change of hereditary forms, should give the work distinction.

If letters are to be carved in raised relief, it must be understood that the proportions of incised letters are quite unsuitable, particularly if the letters are small. Should the same proportions be used, it would be impossible to cut away the stone on either side of the thin strokes, and the serifs, which in incised letters are shaped to a sharp point, could not be formed without chipping the stone. The scale of raised letters should generally be larger and the strokes heavier than those of incised letters. If the inscription in raised letters is of only one or two lines, it may be convenient to cut away the whole surrounding background; but it must be remembered that this

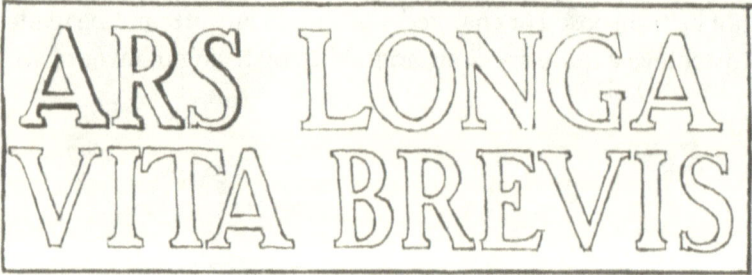

Fig. 20. Inscription in raised relief.

tends to make the letters look thinner than they do in a drawing, just as darkening the background of a drawn inscription reduces the apparent size and thickness of the lettering.

Fig. 21. Inscription in raised relief; only the background is sunk.

For an ordinary tablet inscription on a scale requiring letters perhaps two to three inches high, if the whole background is to be sunk, including the space between the lines of lettering, it is essential to put the lines close together and to keep the letters as compact as possible, in order to avoid a thin and attenuated appearance. The width of the thick strokes should be about one-fifth the height of the letter, although this may

INCISED ROMAN LETTERS

vary somewhat according to the size of the letter; certainly in smallish letters the proportions of incised letters, in which the width of the thick strokes is one-eighth to one-tenth the height of the letters, would be impossible. The serifs must be cut with square ends, as stone is too friable to be cut to sharp points (fig. 20).

I think it is usually better, with raised letters, to sink only the background, leaving the spaces between the lines of letters at surface level. This reduces the sunk area and tends to keep a better proportion between letters and background (fig. 21). As a general rule, the background should not be sunk deeper than the *width* of the thin strokes of the letters, but this is of course contingent on lighting, location of the inscription, and so on.

Fig. 22. Inscription in Gothic lettering.

Gothic lettering is almost invariably best done with the space between lines raised, the descending and ascending strokes of long letters being outlined on the intervening space (fig. 22). This form of lettering derives directly from pen work, and generally the width of a pen stroke is exactly the same as the spaces between.

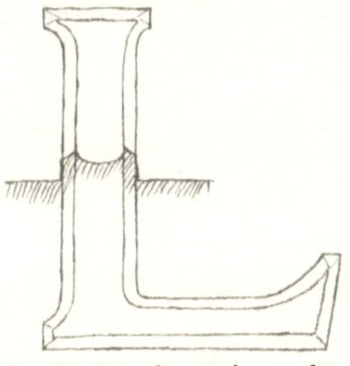

Fig. 23. Raised capital carved in simple section.

If raised capitals are on a sufficiently large scale, an added interest and richness of effect can be obtained by carving the letters to a simple section as shown in figure 23. This requires that the thin strokes of the letters should be wide enough to be so sectioned. Approximately, in a letter 3 inches high the thicks would be about ⅝ inch wide and the thins about ⅜ inch wide, the depth also about ⅜ inch. This sectioned letter is very useful if the lighting is diffused, since the hollow and beveled edges will give an emphasis much greater than that which is given by a flat letter.

CHAPTER 5

Elementary Work in Stone

As an elementary exercise in stone carving, a student may appropriately begin with a simple boss of Gothic foliage. This boss is like myriads of similar ones on any Gothic building, and so long as old buildings are kept in repair, or new buildings are made with any trace of Gothic tradition, foliage like this will be required from stone carvers. In repair work it is usual for the masons to insert the block of new stone into the hollow of the stringcourse, but it is well for a student to accustom himself to such work, and, on simple forms, to learn how to handle tools and to chisel a flat surface.

Figure 24 shows the method of holding the claw chisel (*a*) and the point (*b*). The point, it will be seen, is held at a steeper angle than the chisel because the point is a fracturing tool, whereas the chisel is a surfacing tool. For light work the point should be about 6½ inches long and ⅝ inch in diameter; for heavy work, 8 to 9 inches long and ¾ inch in diameter. The shorter point is more easily controlled, but either should be held firmly in the hand. The hammer used for the point (if the stone is not a very hard one) is 2½ pounds in weight. This is a convenient weight for all work except that on a large scale. The hammer used on this stone (Utah limestone) for the claw chisel is about 1¾ pounds in weight. Practice will enable one to find the appropriate angle of holding and the force of blow to be expended. It should be remembered that each variety of stone requires a different technique of handling, with regard to tools, angle of holding, etc. The heavier hammer has a

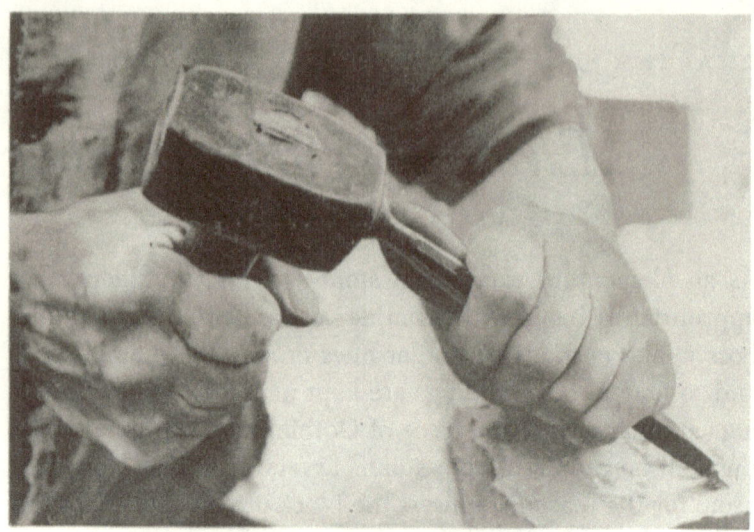

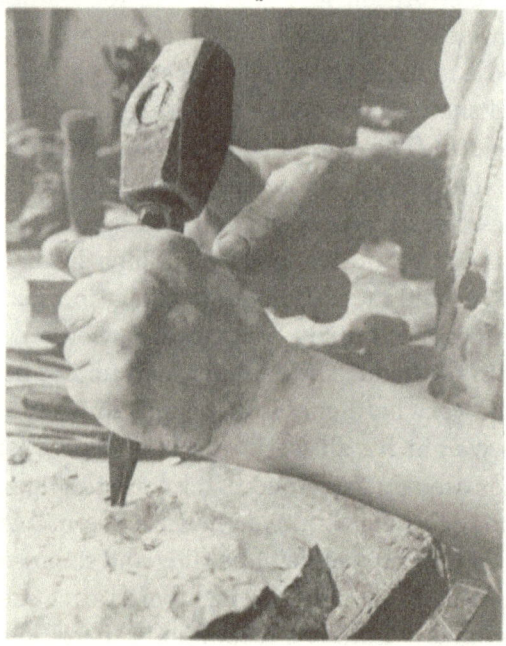

Fig. 24. *a.* The ordinary angle for holding a chisel or claw tool; the smaller, 1¾-pound hammer is shown. *b.* The heavy point, held more nearly vertical than the finishing chisel. The 2½-pound hammer is shown.

ELEMENTARY WORK

Fig. 25. The surface left by the heavy point when used on marble.

slightly longer handle, as it has at times to be used with a swinging blow; the handle in figure 24, *b*, is about 6½ inches long. The lighter hammer handle is only about 5 inches long, as this is used with rather a tapping blow. I mention these lengths because lump hammers are usually sold without handles, and fitting a convenient handle is essential to good workmanship.

It would be advisable to begin carving on any Bath or oölite stone on which rasps can be used. The difficulties are much increased if gritstone is chosen.

54   STONE AND MARBLE CARVING

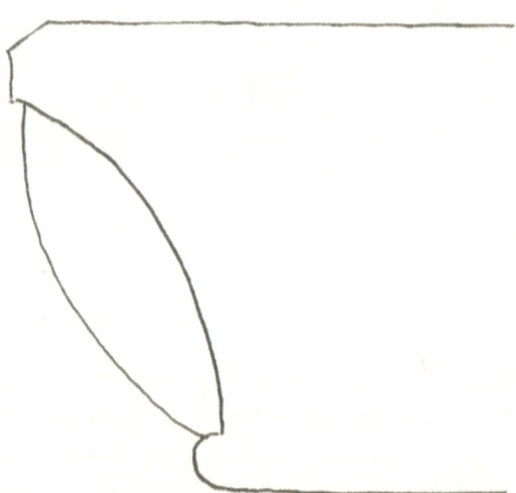

Fig. 26. *Above:* The first stage in shaping the leaf; stone rounded into a simple cushion shape. *Below:* Section.

ELEMENTARY WORK 55

The stringcourse here shown is about 9 by 7 inches; the actual leaf is 6 by 5 inches. Every part of the shaping as shown in figure 26 was done with the point and the wide 1-inch or 1½-inch claw tool and large flat chisel. The surface of the bevel above the leaf was finished with a coarse rasp.

It will be seen that the first state in shaping this leaf is to round it into a simple cushion shape; the next (as shown in fig. 27) is to shape the main contours, a central boss, surrounded by a deep groove. The groove is shallower at the corner (here, the lower right), where the stem of the leaf is to appear. The aim is to get a good variety of surface; also, to use the whole depth of the relief. The shape thus obtained need not be quite smooth, but it should be smooth enough to make contours clearly defined and to allow for drawing the divisions and serrations of the leaf. A drill may conveniently be used on the indented divisions, as it is often easier to chip the stone into a drilled hole, especially when, as here, it has to be deeply sunk. In making the leaf pictured here, I used a small chisel about ¼ inch wide. One must be careful not to undercut until the final shape is achieved.

In the next stage one should outline the central ribs of the leaf and with a gouge cut evenly curved grooves on each side of the midribs and indicate the serrated ends of the leaf. This is the stage at which it is essential to get graceful curves, radiating from the stem of the leaf. It will be seen that although the central boss of the leaf is a large convex shape the midribs are indicated by leaving ridges between two concave shapes, whereas the ends of the leaf are a varied arrangement of convex and concave shapes and sections. In other words, bosses and hollows in pleasant variety are the requisites of any interesting piece of sculpture, and this applies throughout the whole range of work. A boss such as this is usually placed high above the eye, and consequently the cutting should be deep in order to give good shadows. The sections of Gothic foliage

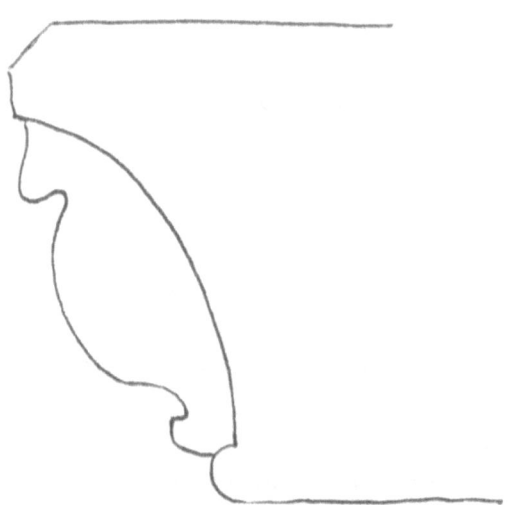

Fig. 27. *Above:* The second stage in shaping the leaf; the main contours of a central boss surrounded by a deep groove have been formed. *Below:* Section.

ELEMENTARY WORK 57

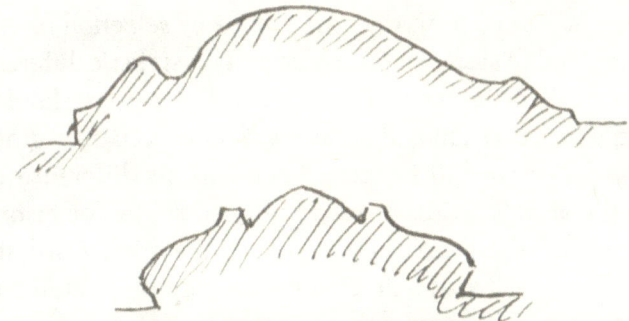

Fig. 28. *Above:* The completed carving. *Middle:* Section down midrib. *Below:* Section across leaf ends.

(and thinking in terms of sections is the first essential for a sculptor) are very generally ogival, as are, for instance, the section longitudinally down the midrib of this leaf and the section over the ends of the leaf, as shown in figure 28. In fact, almost all the lines and sections of the foliage are ogival. The total relief on this boss is about 2 inches, and it is well to use the whole relief, as otherwise the effect is apt to be flat. It is not necessary to sink the interstices of the leaf to the full depth of the curved background, but it is necessary to sink them deep enough to get dark shadows. Indeed, the whole aim in such carving as this is to get a harmonious arrangement of shadow and light. Medieval work similar in kind should be studied and its sections and contours noted, not necessarily because old work should be copied, but in order that its qualities may be understood.

Fig. 29. Cross sections of gouges used in carving the leaf.

The tools used on this carving are as follows: point, large claw tool, smaller ½-inch claw tool, ½-inch chisel, ¼-inch chisel, three gouges sectioned as shown here. No rasps or rifflers are used, except on the bevel above the boss.

It is worth repeating that the choice or selection of every different kind of stone involves also certain stylistic differences in treatment. A fine-grained stone like Caen stone should be treated with precision and delicacy of scale; a coarser-grained one should be treated in accordance with its different qualities and characteristics. A coarse-grained stone, for instance, will not hold sharp arrises, as a fine stone does. Hard stone requires severer treatment. Freestones may be treated freely in every sense. A responsive understanding of the relation of style and scale to material can come only with experience in carving many varieties of stone and ornaments or subjects in many sizes and scales. The foliage sculpture in the Chapter House at Southwell, England, is a beautiful example of stone carving: although it is superficially naturalistic, yet every leaf is shaped with conscious stylism and is exquisitely adapted to a stone technique.

CHAPTER 6

Carving a Portrait in Relief in Limestone

A sculptor may be asked to make a portrait medallion in stone, marble, or alabaster—a portrait of the kind which is set into, or accompanies, a memorial tablet. The methods which I use in carving such a portrait follow.

The first decisions to be made are those concerning the scale, the depth of relief, and the material. A life-size head is likely to look too big unless the carving is to be placed in a very large room or church. As the relief described here was meant to be set over a fireplace in the small library of a private home the scale is about four-fifths life size. The size of the stone is 14 by 12 by 4 inches; the diameter of the circle around the carved head is 11 inches; the head, including beard, is 9½ inches high. The depth of relief is 1¾ inches. The material is limestone.

The carver should prepare a full-size drawing for any portrait. This need not be highly finished, but it must catch the salient characteristics of the person, special care being taken to get the correct facial angle, set of the eye orbit, position of the ear, and the like. Personally, I do not usually make a very elaborate drawing since I prefer to work out the subtleties of the likeness in the carving, but this is a matter for the individual student or sculptor to decide. A study of sculptors' drawings is helpful, particularly the many portrait drawings and etchings of Legros, which all show a preoccupation with the contours of form and ignore local color, i.e., of hair, of iris of the eye, and so on. This is the true sculptor's outlook. An interesting comparison can be made between Legros's drawings and those of his friend and contemporary, Rodin, whose drypoint studies for portrait busts are so vivid and powerful. Rodin seizes all that he can of the sense of life and vitality, while Legros seems consciously to seek out the form and transmute it into a grave and noble stylism. The drawings of Michelangelo are superb examples of sculptor's work and should be reverently studied.

If the portrait is of a living person who is available as a sitter, then, of course, the drawing should be made directly from life, and some measurements may be found useful. But medallion portraits are commonly of deceased persons and as a rule have to be carved from photographs or paintings. The relief of Browning used here as an example was done from a photograph and from a reproduction of the portrait by Watts in the National Portrait Gallery, London.

The first illustration (fig. 30) shows, at the left, the stone after it has been worked on with the pitcher; the width of the tool (about ⅞ inch) may be traced in the marks around the edges. The pitcher is not a chisel and has a thick and heavy beveled edge, which does not cut the stone, but fractures it. It is held against any square, or nearly square, edge, and should be struck sharply with a heavyish hammer—a blow quite different from the steady tapping blows on the point or the chisels. It will be seen in the reproduction that the pitcher has broken the stone beyond the penciled outline at the top of the head. This is of no account, as the relief is not here at full height. When as much as possible of the background has been removed by the pitcher, the point should be used to clear away the excess stone. Then use a claw tool as large as is convenient—here, 1½ inches wide—and work over the whole area (ignoring the further depth of the circle), getting the back-

A PORTRAIT IN RELIEF

ground approximately level, as on the right side in figure 30. There is no need of keeping an exact edge all around the outline of the head. Many people seem to think that the shape of the head and profile should be accurately set down to the

Fig. 30. First stage of relief portrait. Only the pitcher (*left*) and the 1½-inch claw tool (*right*) have been used.

depth required. This would make the first stage look as if the head were fret-cut to an exact outline and applied to a flat background, but this would be difficult to do and would waste a great deal of time, for the full depth of the relief is required only at one point above the ear, and the general disposition of parts should be shown as early as possible. The actual outline is not more important than the first shaping of the structure of the face; indeed, it is less important. The essential thing is to grasp and record as clearly as possible the salient structural characteristics of the head. The final definition of the outline is not made until the whole head is shaped. It is the cumula-

Fig. 31. Second stage of relief portrait. Almost all the work has been done with the claw tool shown at the left, which has four teeth and is about ¾-inch wide.

tive effect of bringing all the parts and aspects of a piece of sculpture into true relation that alone can produce a work of art. The sense of likeness resides in the relation of all the parts to the whole rather than merely in an accurate profile. For that reason the sculptor should avoid small subtleties and seek for the general structure of the face and the relative proportions of the features.

A PORTRAIT IN RELIEF 63

Figure 31 shows the forms roughly shaped with the coarse claw tool, about 1 inch wide, which is shown there; it will be seen that the full relief is kept in only two places. The circle is lightly indicated and the position of the features and beard are marked, although not yet definitely. In a relief portrait the profile aspect is in true scale, while the front view—the carving seen edgewise—is narrowed into the depth of the relief. If the head were in such high relief as to be just half the head in the round, the depth would be nearly four inches. Actually, it is less than half this, but the aim should be to keep the same ratio in the disposition of the features in the relief.

When looked at edgewise, the likeness should be clear, although in that aspect all the dimensions are narrowed. Therefore, as work proceeds, keep looking at it not only from the front (in the carving, profile) aspect, but also look carefully at it from the edge (in the carving, front view). It is well to allow ample projection for the hair and ear, in this carving perhaps ½ inch. If too much margin is allowed, it can easily be reduced, but if too little, one may be involved in lowering and so re-carving the whole face in order to get sufficient relief for the hair. (This is less important when the relief is very shallow, in which case careful drawing must give the suggestion of the contour. See, for instance, the portrait on a coin, where the impression of contour is mainly given by the drawing.)

Figure 33 shows the development of the portrait, only claw tools as yet being used. The relief allowed for the hair is clearly shown. The size and disposition of the ear is defined, and the orbit of the eye is characteristically marked, as is the muscle between nose and mouth.

The loose definition of the shape of the head and hair leaves one some scope for changes, if any be required; that is, if one cuts too much off the outline of the face, the whole profile can be brought into its true relation again by a very slight narrowing of the head. The definition around the nostrils and the eye

Fig. 32. *a.* Full relief as in nature. *b.* Sculptured relief, reduced in depth but keeping the same ratio between the different parts. *c.* The essentials of the portrait, which lie in the relationship of a group of lines, not in the outline of the profile.

is not yet sharply incised, and the indication of the mouth and beard is still tentative. The outline avoids the sharp final definition. It will be seen that the claw tools used for the face have smaller teeth than those used in the earlier stages. One is a bullnosed claw chisel; the other is a ½-inch chisel with four cuts and five teeth, and although it is much worn, so that the

A PORTRAIT IN RELIEF

teeth do not leave deep indentations, it must be kept perfectly sharp at all times. Care should be taken throughout the work that the tools do not get blunted. Chiseling over shells, fossils, or other flaws in the stone (visible on the brow in this relief),

Fig. 33. Third stage of relief portrait. The characteristics of the features and their disposition in relation to one another are being defined, finer claw tools being used. No sharp definition; no undercutting.

may cause a good deal of blunting of the fine claws, but whenever a tool shows any signs of not cutting a clean surface, it should be sharpened at once. No amount of care taken to keep the tools in perfect condition can be too great. It is never possible to get stone entirely free from shells and other flaws—whenever these are come upon, they must be dealt with carefully and deliberately.

Figure 34 shows more searching study of the modeling of the face. The profile, although still unfinished, has been worked over, and the shaping of the main contours of the beard and tufts of hair has been begun. It will be seen that no attempt is

Fig. 34. Fourth stage of relief portrait. Closer and more searching modeling of features; ear indicated, and the hair shaped in tufts. The face has been worked over with fine claw tools in which the gaps are almost worn out; the profile is more clearly defined. Still no undercutting. The circular inset has, on the right, been sunk to almost its final depth by the use of a smooth chisel, and the even thickening of the block has been started at the edges.

made to make the hair "hairy." It has been translated into a form suitable to a chiseled technique, although it follows closely the disposition of the tufts of hair in the National Gallery portrait. The slab of stone is reduced to approximately its

A PORTRAIT IN RELIEF 67

final thickness around the edges, and the final depth of background within the circle is more or less fixed. The definition of the circle is, of course, impossible until the entire surface of the corners is smoothly chiseled. The convolutions of the ear are indicated, and it will be seen that there are traces of the worn claw tools everywhere over the face. Indeed, I rarely use a smooth chisel until the very last stages. The traces of the worn claw tools are not unpleasant and they help to give a sense of direction to the forms. In the treatment of hair and beard it will be observed that the tufts of hair have a definite shape before the incisions are put in to mark the growth and direction. Again, as with the forms of the face, it is essential to get the general shape before getting the detail. The tendency to indicate detail early must be disciplined into subjection. This is partly because working on detail too soon is wasteful of time; also, because the larger general contours are more important and more essential, although they are less easily seen. Power to see beyond detail to general shape comes only with experience and should be steadily cultivated.

Figure 35 shows the finished relief. The surface of the corners has been chiseled and then rasped smooth to give a good surface for the lettering. The inset circle has been deepened to about ⅜ inch, which helps to integrate the composition; without that circle the area surrounding the head would be too great and the general design would be too diffused. It will be seen that the area of the head itself is greater than the area of background within the circle. This is usually a safe rule, as study of good medals and medallions will corroborate. Unless there is some special reason for it, not much of the shoulder should be shown, as this tends to create difficulty in respect to the depth of the relief and almost inevitably enlarges the area of the background and makes a proportionate reduction in the scale of the head. Of course, medallion or relief portraits are not necessarily circular; and for each the shape and composition must be decided either as part of a larger scheme or on its own merits as a piece of designing.

It will be seen that in the finished carving the proportions of the block of stone seem different. In the earlier stages the block looks nearly square, whereas in the final stage it looks

Fig. 35. Finished relief, with name in incised Roman capitals, and dates.

distinctly rectangular. This results from the smoothing of all the area except the head, and is just another evidence that proportion is not readily reducible to rules, but is a matter of relativity and even of illusion. The scale of the lettering and dates is a problem susceptible of several solutions. To divide the name into two syllables seemed better than to reduce the letters to a scale that would have accommodated the whole name on one line, as this would have made a great disparity between the scale of the head and of the lettering.

CHAPTER 7

Carving a Child's Head in Marble

The task of carving a head in marble should not be attempted until one has had a good deal of experience with softer and more tractable stones, but marble is a beautiful medium, and ultimately almost every carver desires to use it. I am here describing as closely as possible the process of carving the bust of a child directly from a block of Carrara marble. One good reason against working in marble before one has some mastery of the technique of carving in stone is that marble is much more costly than any freestone, and, being hard in texture, is much slower and more hazardous to work. It is also strangely brittle and the cost of a breakage is three or four times that of stone, both in time and material.

The block required for this bust was about 14 by 8 by 7 inches, and it had to be cut from an old marble stair tread about 3 feet long and 14 inches wide. No emery or other power saw being available, I faced the problem of deciding whether to rig up a grub saw and try to get a mason to help cut off the required block, which would probably have taken a day at least, or to chisel a deep "chase" (as it is called) around the block and fracture off a piece of the desired size. I decided on this and, with the heavy point, cut a rough V groove round the block. This took me about three hours (the block, having lain in the yard for thirty-five years, was very dry and brittle); and then, using the heavier (2½-pound) hammer, struck a sharp blow on the chisel, which was held tightly against the bottom of the groove, and broke off the piece required. The small block, roughly the required size, then weighed about 60 pounds. Luckily the fracture kept very even, as may be seen

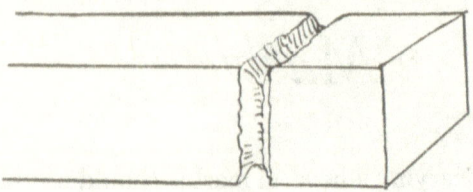

Fig. 36. Method of fracturing a large block of stone, by means of a V chase.

in figure 42 (p. 76); but marble, being crystalline and with no bed, is incalculable, and it is not advisable to risk a very wide fracture. Here, the V chase being nearly 2 inches deep on each side, the fracture was rather less than half the distance through. Another method is to cut a chase, say about 1 inch deep, and then drill five or six holes about another inch deep and ½ inch in diameter in the bottom of the chase and, using what are called "feathers and wedges" (fig. 37), tap the wedges alternately a little at a time; with reasonable luck the fracture will follow straight through.

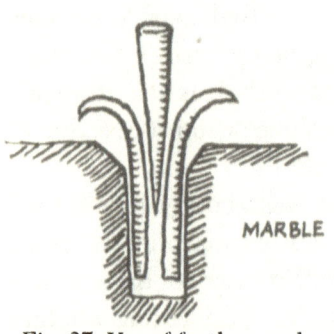

Fig. 37. Use of feathers and wedge in fracturing.

Of course none of this is applicable if the student can go to a marble yard and have a block cut to the required size with a power saw. For the head discussed here, it would have been cut as shown in figure 38. But that is not always possible, so I mention these other methods and devices. A student must learn to be adaptable and as independent of machinery as is possible. The height of the block—14 inches—allows 4 or 5

A CHILD'S HEAD

inches at the base for fixing into a wooden frame so that it is held fast (for stone or marble cannot be held in a vise or by clamps, as wood is fixed for carving). The rough shaping as shown in figure 42 was done before fixing, by steadying the block against a larger block of stone, and except for the rabbeted surface at the base the work was all done with a pitcher

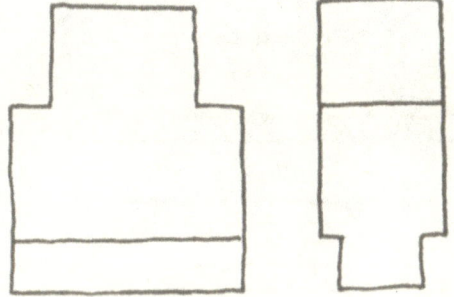

Fig. 38. Front and side elevations of block of marble prepared with power saw.

and a heavy point. It is well to do this before fixing since to do so afterward puts a severe strain on any box or other device used for fastening. A rabbet, about 3 inches in height and 1¼ inches in depth, was cut along the base, at front and back, and around this were fitted four substantial pieces of wood. (See fig. 39.)

All this may seem elaborate, but it is essential to have the block steady, and when one is working smallish blocks the manner of fixing them is important. The hazards of carving marble are many. It is well not to increase them by attempting to carve an insecurely fixed block.

For really small carvings in marble there is another method of fixing. After shaping as much as possible (about to the stage shown in fig. 42), set it in a bed of wet plaster of Paris laid on a heavy block of stone, and pack strips of "scrim," or open-meshed canvas, which have been dipped in plaster, tightly around the base. Care must be taken that both the marble and

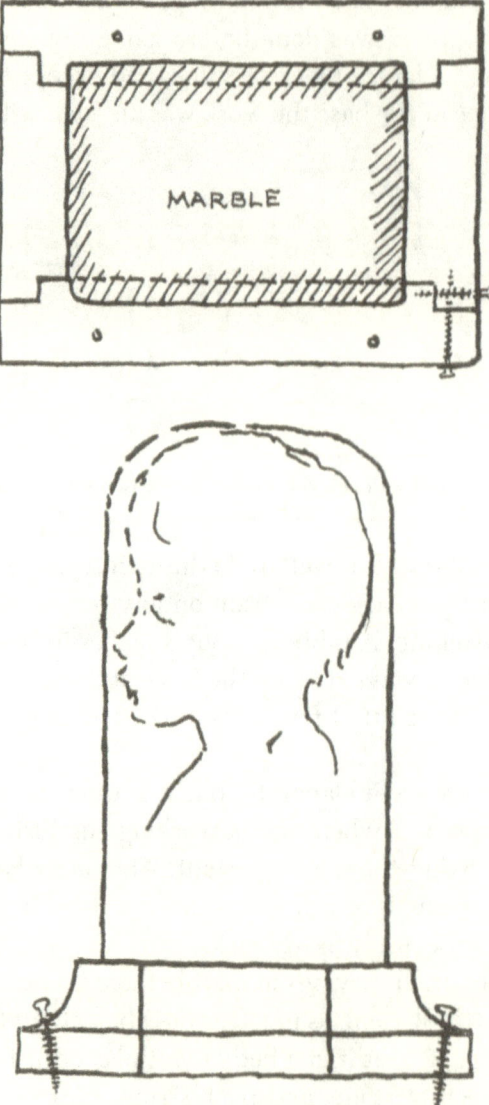

Fig. 39. *Above*, wooden frame for fixing marble while carving; *below*, end view, with screws used to fasten box to bench.

A CHILD'S HEAD

the stone are clean and wet before the bed of plaster is laid and the packing is done. The top surface of the stone should be roughened; a soft, rather absorbent stone is best. The advantage of the box method is that the marble is removable and can be taken out and replaced as required. The student will find, by experiment, the convenient working height. The top of the head discussed here was about 4 feet 9 inches from the floor—a convenient level for a person like myself, about 5 feet 6 inches tall. The level should be kept high rather than low as it is tiring to have to stoop. It is always possible to stand on a block.

It is necessary to consider these details since difficulties in fixing work are constantly arising and it is only when working on a scale greater than half life size for a figure, and about life size for a head-and-shoulders bust, that blocks remain steady by their own weight—a great convenience in carving. A useful bench height is 40 to 42 inches. A mason's banker is much lower—usually only 24 to 27 inches,—but a mason ordinarily works on the horizontal surface of the stone only, and not, as the sculptor does, on its vertical surfaces.

Here, I am describing the process of direct carving of a portrait. The subject being only 18 or 20 months old, "posing" in the sense of sitting still was impossible. I made several small sketches, watched the child constantly to note individual characteristics, and took a few measurements with calipers, as shown in the rough outlines of front and profile (fig. 40). If a student is copying from a clay or plaster model, the actual carving process is exactly the same as if one were working from a living model, i.e., the process is one of gradual attrition of the material from a rough and general contour to fine and particular detail.

In practice, I think it is usually better to work rather under life size. A life-size marble head in a room of ordinary dimensions looks very large; hence I reduced the size of the head from 8 inches to 6½ inches. The head then is about four-fifths life size. The simplest way to get all one's measurements in the same ratio is to make a scale on an angle (see fig. 41); here, one side of the angle was 8 inches long, the other 6½ inches. Join the ends and, after marking on the longer, full-size line, the

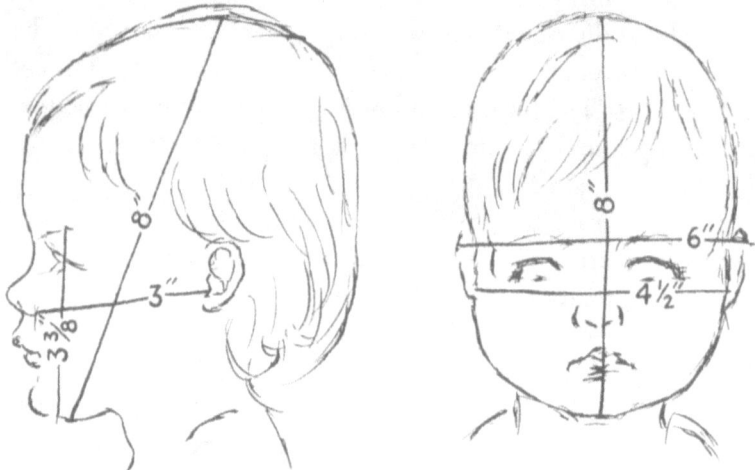

Fig. 40. Typical preliminary sketches giving salient measurements.

several measurements taken from the child, run parallels to the shorter line, and the measurements will be in exact ratio. The only measuring instruments required are calipers, compasses, and a foot rule. In practice, about six head measurements are useful:

1. Chin to top of head.
2. Depth from nose tip, or from brow, to back of head.
3. Width across ears, or, if ears are hidden, across hair.
4. Width across malar (cheek) bones.
5. From chin to eyebrows. This includes all the features and can be subdivided into two parts, usually nearly equal, chin to nose and nose to eyebrows.
6. From the wing of nose to orifice of ear. A useful measurement when working on the side view of the head.

A CHILD'S HEAD

Smaller measurements may be taken: width of mouth or nose; length of ear, and so on; but too much reliance should not be placed on measurements. The sculptor's eye, which is the final test, must be exercised and trusted, in order to develop the sense of form.

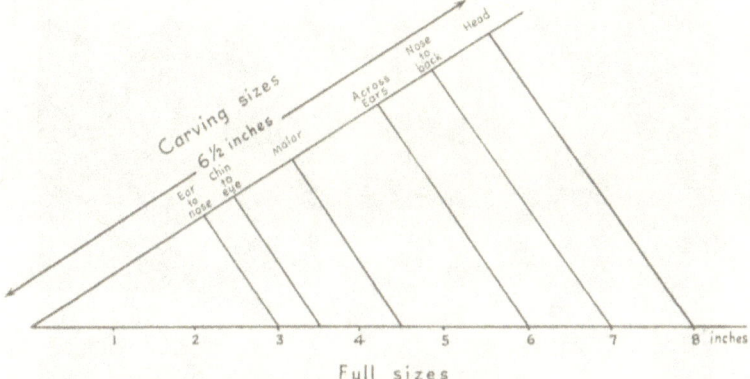

Fig. 41. Scale for reducing 8-inch head for 6½-inch carving.

Stage I

The marble, having been roughly shaped (as shown in fig. 42), should be placed in its box fastening and this should be clamped or screwed to the bench. The first step is to shape the simple ovoid of the head, using first the point, then the ½-inch claw tool. Experience alone will tell what the force of the hammer blows, and the size and scale of the chippings, should be. Marble should be cut with care and deliberation. Impetuosity in chiseling will inevitably bring trouble. Persistent, slow attrition will achieve the form better, and even more quickly, than vehement chiseling. The ovoid shape should be fairly even and symmetrical, but not cut too close to the exact size. Some margin should be allowed; in this scale, perhaps ⅜ to ½ inch. Particularly, there should be ample depth (nose to back of head), so that if some slight changes are required in the features there is room to cut back and make the necessary modifications.

Fig. 42. The block for the bust, cut from large block and roughly shaped with the point before fixing into wooden box. Base has been rabbetted for fixing.

A CHILD'S HEAD

The next step is to shape the facial angle, a very decided factor in a likeness. (The facial angle of a child is quite distinct from that of an adult.) This fixes the position of the tip of the nose, and from that the position of the eyes and mouth can be noted and indicated by shallow and tentative depressions. No sharp definition should be aimed at. The eye sockets should be kept just the least bit low in the head, for it is always possible to cut a little off the top of the head, or use it in hair, whereas, if the eyes are set even a fraction too high, it is difficult to rectify the mistake. Still, modifications can be made so long as one has depth from back to front, although, of course, the further the carving proceeds the less desirable it is to have to lose the work and cut farther back to adjust the features. No cutting under the chin should be done until the disposition of the features is clearly made. It is surprising how the likeness begins to appear even when there is hardly more than a mere suggestion of the spacing of the features, which should be, at this stage, just the least bit larger than they will be in the finished bust.

Of course it is not possible to keep every feature slightly large, because the controlling shape is already approximately right in size and therefore the enlargement of one feature involves a reduction in the adjoining parts; but it is essential to avoid getting the nose thin, or the eyes too near together. A good way to avoid getting detail too early in the work is to use only relatively large tools. All the shaping of the face in figure 43 was done with a ½-inch claw tool, and no detailed work is possible with such a tool. It is essential to adhere closely to the scale on which the work was planned. The whole portrait is in the space between chin and eyebrows vertically, and within the width of the malar bones horizontally (here, a space of about 4 by 4½ inches); hence it should not be difficult for a student of some experience to seize and hold the relative scale of each feature within this small area.

Fig. 43. The first day's work; all shaping done with ½-inch claw tool. The rabbetted base is here covered by the box in which the block is fastened.

Do not undercut the chin until later. Apart from the question of strength, delay this deep incision until it is quite certain that the features are all disposed in their proper relation and scale. It will be seen from figure 43 that at this stage it looks impossible that the shoulders could come within the

A CHILD'S HEAD 79

block. Yet actually in the finished work the shoulders are not as wide as the block. The aim, throughout stage I, is to seize on the character of the model and to grasp clearly the scale of the head. With these in your mind, proceed toward more definition.

Stage II

This is perhaps the most important stage in the work, for now the tentative suggestion of the features has to give place to more exact definition. The essentials of each feature, the contours of the nose and nostrils, the disposition and set of the eyes, the curves, and, above all, the character of the mouth, have all to be observed and recorded; yet not as separate forms, but as together making the distinctive personality of the model. Naturally this requires some psychological understanding as well as technical skill. The perception of those subtle differences in features which distinguish this sitter from what might be called the norm is possible only to one with some experience and power of draftsmanship. If one cannot draw a likeness, it is certain one cannot carve one.

Two or three more tools are now necessary (though the point and ½-inch claw continue to be used for rough work); the use of these may be clearly traced in figure 44. Actually, I used two exactly similar claw tools, substantially rigid, each about ⅝ inch wide and with two cuts (three teeth). It is always convenient to have two or three to avoid constant sharpening. They *must* be kept sharp. The third tool was also a claw tool, but although it was only about ⅝ inch wide it had four cuts (five teeth). Its marks may be clearly seen on the brow above the right eye of the head. It is convenient to grind this tool to a slightly bullnosed shape. So ground, it can be used more like a gouge (none of the tools used so far have been gouges).

If figure 44 be compared with figure 55 (the finished head, p. 100), it will be seen that it is in this early stage that the personal characteristics which make the likeness are seized on,

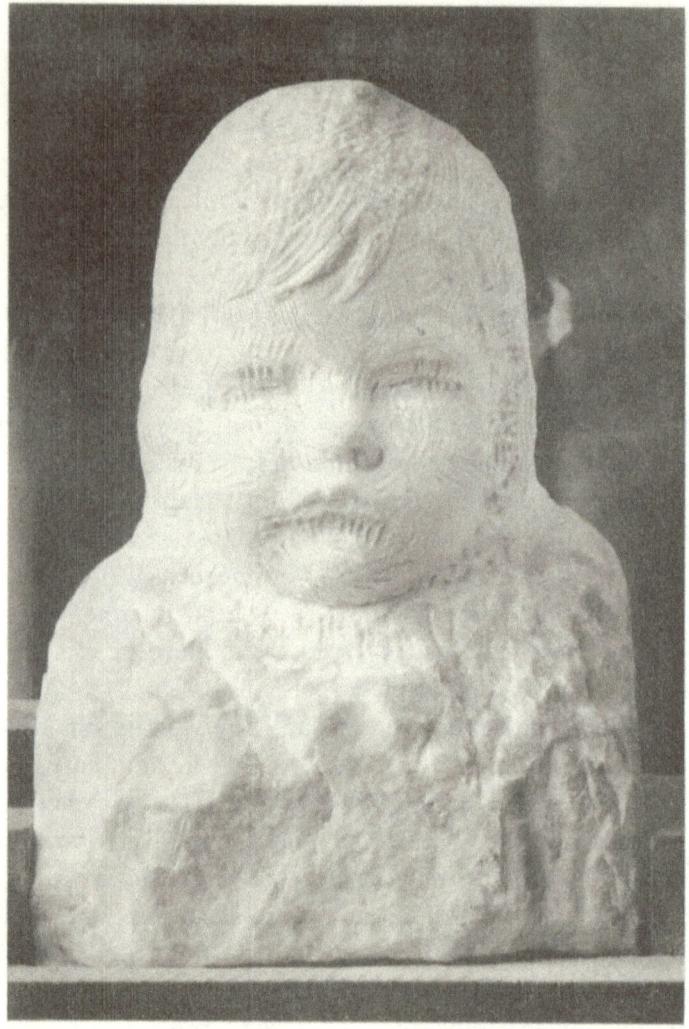

Fig. 44. The beginnings of the real portrait; expression of character. Note the varying direction of claw-tool cuts, which are balanced more or less symmetrically on each side of the face.

A CHILD'S HEAD

and, although the carving is very general, there is a clear statement of personality. Note, too, how the direction of the chisel marks gives expressiveness to the form. No rules can be given (any more than one can give a student painter directions about brushwork), but practice will give a student a feeling for form and for the most expressive way of defining it.

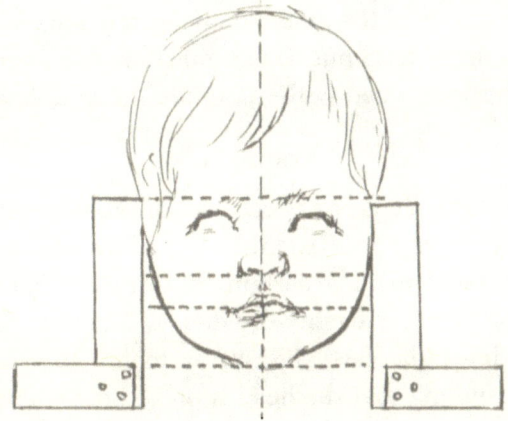

Fig. 45. Testing the even division of the face with two squares. The four main divisions of the face are also indicated.

The one rule to be observed is to avoid all undercutting, and indeed all sharp and incisive definition, until one is quite sure of the right relation of all the component parts of the head, balanced with reasonable symmetry. The personality which makes a good portrait is more likely to be expressed in the relative disposition of parts than in minor details, and it is necessary to guard against the desire to get to work on the detail. Once the width across the malar bones has been defined, allowing only a margin of ⅛ inch to ¼ inch, the four divisions of the face should be clearly decided (see fig. 45), as should also the approximate size and position of the ears (which are much farther back than most beginners realize—see figure 40, p. 74). I cannot too strongly urge that one should never cut behind the ears, or undercut the wings of the nose, or define the eyes, or cut any indication of the nostrils, or undercut the chin, until the whole head is shaped and the portrait is a recognizably good likeness. Any sharp incisions or undercutting will surely hamper one in working the features into what they must finally become: not only a portrait, but also a harmonious arrangement of bosses and hollows. The shape of the eyes, or curves of the mouth, may be indicated with pencil, as a preliminary test, but a recognizable and characteristic likeness can be reached with the minimum of definition. (See fig. 44.)

Stage III

It is well at this stage to check measurements and test the work for symmetry and balance. A few devices are helpful. The simplest way to make certain, for instance, that the width across malar bones is evenly divided by a medial line drawn in pencil down the face (fig. 46) is to use two carpenter's squares—assuming that the head is on a vertical axis and that the bench is reasonably horizontal (fig. 45). This medial line should be constantly renewed. It is also useful to look at the head upside down, when faults of asymmetry are more easily seen; also, as portrait painters do, to look at it in a mirror. Even after very long experience in such work, I seldom fail to find some strange inequality in balance when first the work is held in front of a mirror. A curious but I think incontrovertible fact is that if the artist has himself a facial asymmetry (and few faces are perfectly balanced), it tends to be repeated in the process of carving any head. I mention this without attempting to explain it.

Strips of thin cardboard or, better still, of very thin zinc are useful for winding around the head to make certain, for instance, that the ears are level. Indeed, they are often useful for measuring on contours, where a rule is useless. A tape measure is also handy. There is an architect's instrument, for

A CHILD'S HEAD

Fig. 46. The four horizontal divisions of the face (see fig. 45) clearly defined; the scale and sizes fixed, leaving only a narrow margin. Ears indicated. No undercutting anywhere, not even in the mouth. The penciled medial line is an aid in getting symmetry.

Fig. 47. The disposition of the tufts of hair has been begun; the profile has been defined; and the position of the ears in relation to the curves of the hair and the contours of the face has been determined. The head is supported on a wide expanse of marble, with a buttress at both front and back; no attempt at defining the neck has been made.

A CHILD'S HEAD

taking profiles of moldings, which can be pressed against the face; the thin metal laminations follow the contours, and hence asymmetry is readily seen. But it cannot be too insistently said that the eye is still the best, as it is the most accessible, measuring device, and the more it is used for that purpose the better it becomes as an instrument. It is well to equalize as nearly as possible the work on the two sides of a head. A right-

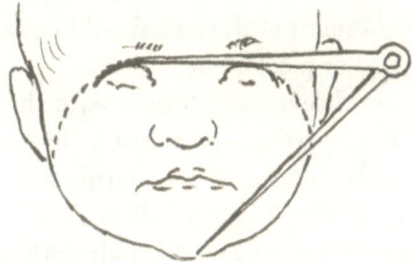

Fig. 48. Testing the symmetry of the eyes with a compass centered on the chin.

handed person is likely to work more easily on the right side of a face. This should be guarded against and both sides should be kept at the same stage. It is a great convenience to acquire, by practice, the habit of working either right- or left-handedly. Indeed, this ability is almost essential and, however difficult at first, should be persistently practiced until it becomes easy.

The position of the ears should be roughly indicated at an early stage in the carving, since they mark the limit of the area of the face in side view, but the sculptor should do no more than determine their approximate size and position until the face itself is clearly defined. He should make no attempt at shaping the convolutions; above all, should not cut behind the ears or sharply define their size and shape. (See fig. 47.) In balancing the eyes, it is sometimes useful to set compasses on the chin and draw a line through the outer corners of the eyes, continuing the line down the cheek, where it usually falls a little below the base of the ears. (See fig. 48.)

The treatment of hair is important, for not only is the area of hair generally considerably larger than that of the face, but hair has its characteristic shape, texture, and growth, all of which must be recorded in portraiture. It is essential to distinguish between the appropriate and characteristic treatment of hair in modeling and the distinct and entirely different treatment which is suitable in carving. Therefore, if one is making a modeled head as preliminary to carving it in stone or marble, the treatment of the hair should be that of carving, and not a thumbed or plastic one.

This book is not directly concerned with the technique of modeling, but it is perhaps permissible to suggest that in making a clay or plastic model for a marble head the best way to get a real sense of chiseling is to allow the clay to get about half hardened and then to carve the hair with wire modeling tools. Thus there will be less discrepancy between the two processes, and the result will probably be better. It would be well for a student to study examples of hair treatment in marble or stone, especially such as were done before sculptors were so rigidly divided into modelers and carvers. Greek and Greco-Roman portraits offer admirable examples. So, too, do the best medieval sculptures, where no trace of modeling ever intrudes on the chiseled stone; instead, there are crisp incisions and sharp definition.

The hair on the child's head here illustrated was naturally thin and wispy and the treatment had to suggest this quality while retaining the feeling of the chisel and the marble. The difference in texture of hair from skin can be suggested by working the hair mostly with toothed tools. Here, after the early stages, the hair was wholly worked with tools in which the cuts forming the teeth were almost worn out and therefore left very slight marks. The main dispositions of the tufts and direction of growth should be indicated fairly early in the work. The hair should not be left a heavy mass to be carved

A CHILD'S HEAD

after the face is entirely finished; it enters into the design of the head, and its curves and contours can be composed into a harmonious relationship with the face and features. All the rough shaping of the hair should be done while the head rests secure on a solid basis of uncut marble. (See figs. 44, 46, and 47.) In my portrait, the buttress at the back of the neck remained until all the hair was worked over in detail, to the stage shown in figure 54 (p. 98), which also shows a corresponding buttress supporting the chin. Both these supports to the neck must remain until the last stages of the work. To remove them too early is to invite trouble and risk breakage.

Personally, I find that if one's perceptions and one's eyes become tired with searching out and carving subtle details of the face, it is well to turn to work on the hair or do preliminary work on the shoulders, as less exacting. It must not be forgotten that, besides the physical labor of chiseling hard stone, which, though exhilarating, is tiring to the wrists and cramping to the fingers, there is also the equally essential exercising of the perceptive faculties, and no good work can be done when these are tired or exhausted.

Stage IV

I have already mentioned that toothed tools are at their best for doing subtle contours when the cuts forming the teeth are almost worn out, and it is in these later stages of work that they are most useful. It is now also necessary to have some finer-toothed tools, both bullnosed and, if one can procure them or make them, toothed gouges. It is difficult to explain why toothed tools seem more responsive under the hand as one works over subtle contours, but it certainly is so; and the further the work proceeds the more delicate become the distinctions which must be made. Every contour has to be analyzed if one is to find its shape and to decide where a convex form changes to a concave one, and the area and shape of each

Fig. 49. The hair has been shaped as far as possible without removing the buttress at the back of the neck. The block has been withdrawn from the box fastening.

A CHILD'S HEAD

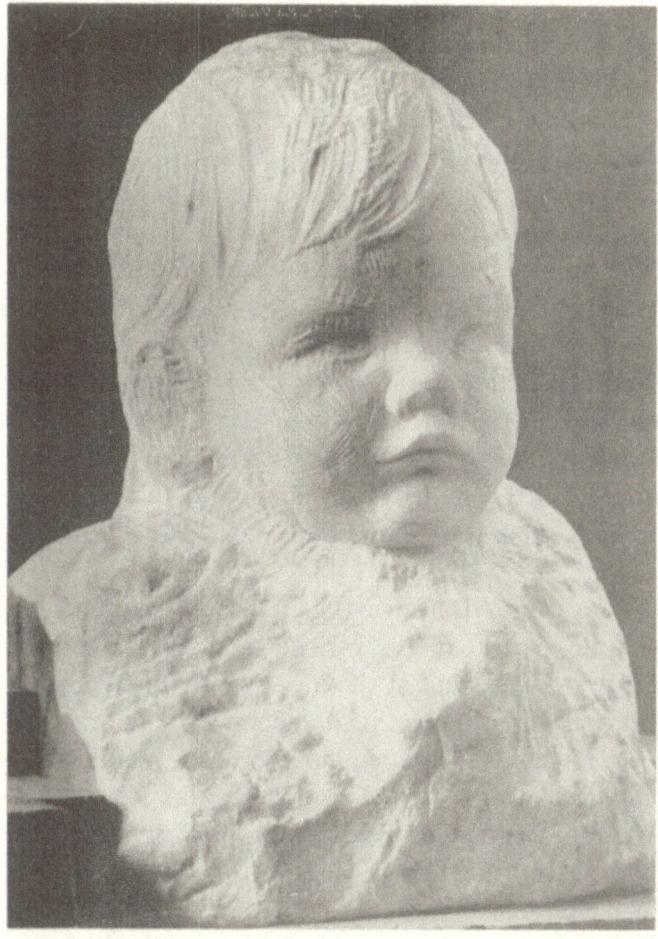

Fig. 50. The contours of the face have been worked with claw tools, nearly worn out; the nostrils have been indicated, and the eyes lightly defined, but there is still no undercutting. The penciled medial line has been renewed.

must be distinguished. In the previous stages the forms have been general, but now they have to be more particularized; this means using a greater variety of delicate tools, more thinly ground. Several gouges are required. These should be carefully sharpened on a carborundum or similar stone, and they must be kept as sharp as wood-carving tools. Traces of this use are visible around the mouth and nostrils (fig. 50), but it will be seen that almost all convex forms have been shaped with rather fine-toothed tools. The marks of coarser claw tools may be seen in the hair and the ear. In figure 47 is shown the disposition of the hair; also the manner in which some of its masses echo the curve of the brow and touch and support the ear. The profile should be carefully studied and made as accurate as possible. This is the time to use finely ground toothed tools, especially such as are nearly worn out, ground thin and sharpened to a fine edge. I prefer to carry the work almost to the very last stage before using smooth chisels; the faint marks of worn claw tools are so slight that they may even enhance the interest of the surface. If a really smooth surface is preferred, these marks are easily removed with rifflers or emery cloth.

The forms around the eyes (fig. 51) must be studied and the upper eyelid indicated. This varies a good deal. Sometimes the lid is not visible except at the inner corner of the eye; more often it is visible at both inner and outer corners, and, in some children, it may be seen throughout its whole length, although this may make a child's eye look rather old. The student must study carefully all such details, both by observation and, if need be, by drawing, and it is essential also for him to note the axis on which the eyes are set. Occasionally it is horizontal, but more often it is at a slight angle which may tilt either inward or outward. I find that making small studies of such details is an aid to memory, even if one does not actually copy them, or even look at them again. Such studies make it possible for a careful observer to note in a few moments, details which may take many hours to record in the marble.

The under eyelid is much less sharply defined than the upper. It must also be noted that the eye is globular and that therefore the section across the eye from corner to corner is

A CHILD'S HEAD

also the section for the shorter distance between the upper and the lower lids. An inexperienced student will almost always carve this section wrong. The indication of the iris of the eye demands thoughtful attention. Some artists insist that, as this is a matter of color and not of form, the iris should not be represented in sculpture at all. It is true that in many ex-

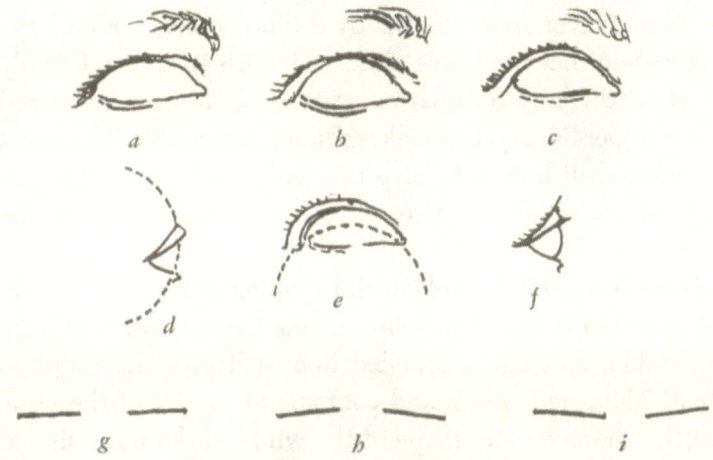

Fig. 51. Forms of the eye. *a.* Upper lid on inner corner only. *b.* Upper lid at outer and inner corner. *c.* Upper lid throughout its length. *d.* Section of eyeball, a globe, from the side. *e.* Section of eyeball from the front. *f.* Incorrect section of eye—a common error. *g–i.* Axis of eyes: horizontal; normal; slightly slanted.

amples of classical sculpture the iris is not carved, but it should not be forgotten that nearly all this sculpture was originally painted and that therefore there was less need to mark this detail by carving. The same is true of medieval sculptures, and the fact that these do not show carved incisions does not mean that the iris was not shown by painting. I think it is chiefly a question of style. If the carving is being done in a realistic manner, I think the iris may be represented by carving; if, however, the work is being done in a rather stylized manner, perhaps it is more appropriate to omit this touch of realism.

No final rule can be laid down. Each work must be considered as a separate problem and the authority of great artists may be invoked for either method. As Shaw remarks, "The only golden rule is that there is no golden rule." Both Bernini and Houdon devised expressive ways of representing eyes, and a student may be advised to make a careful study of their methods, both from casts and photographs. One warning may be given. Never show the iris by drilling a deep round hole. It is seldom that the whole circle of the iris is visible. Usually about a fifth, or even a quarter, of its circumference is covered by the upper lid, and this makes drilling impossible. The effect of such a drill hole is to give the sculptured eye a very unpleasant stare. (In surprise or fear, the whole iris *may* be visible.)

There is a good deal of careful shaping to be done around the nose, but it is well to delay cutting the nostrils. A shallow depression, or even a penciled line, will give the required effect. The small bevels and contours at the tip of the nose, and the characteristic shape of the wings of the nose, should be studied. The definition of the hair on the brow and around the ears should now be marked, but care must be taken that these incisions be not too deeply cut until the final touches are given to the carving.

Shaping the eyes leads naturally to consideration of the orbit of the eye, the ridge of the frontal bone, the malar bone, and thence to the ears. These should be carefully studied, the student observing from the front view how they project and noting the farthest projection from the cheek. A careful drawing should be made of the ear as seen from the side, and any peculiarities of structure or shape should be noted. It is practically impossible to carve the ear as thin as it is in nature, but since in a child it is usually supported by hair, something like its characteristic shape can be achieved. A fiddle drill, or an ordinary hand drill, may be useful for doing this work, and

A CHILD'S HEAD

drill holes may lessen the risk of breakage by chiseling. The delicate work should be done with very sharp small chisels and gouges, using the light dummy. In carving marble, or any of the harder stones, no work can be done by pushing the tools (as in wood carving or in soft stone), and one has to learn to do even the most delicate work with care and precision, using the dummy or a light (1½ pound) hammer.

It is often useful, although it may seem strange, to remove the head from its fastening and work on it upside down! From this unusual angle any asymmetry is more easily seen. Particularly, this is useful in balancing the eyes and the nose, and again the mirror should be used to aid in effecting symmetry.

Occasionally, small convex surfaces, as in the nose and ears, may be carved by using gouges inverted. This can only be done with gouges that are not deeply curved, but at times it is a useful method. In analyzing the forms, care must be taken to distinguish between accidental and minute contours and the essential and structural contours. This distinction can only come by practice, but the fact that a good likeness can be achieved with very simple forms should show one that good portraiture does not necessarily require minutiae.

Before work is begun on the shoulders, the hair should be done as completely as possible, although the buttress at the back of the neck must be left as it is; for it would be risky to do anything but the lightest work on the hair once the neck is reduced to its proper size. Figure 52 shows the head almost completely carved, yet the shoulders so unshaped that the block looks too narrow to contain them. The shaping of the shoulders should be done from the deltoids, and from there the collar bone should be followed as far as possible without removing the buttress from the chest to the chin, though this may be carefully reduced in width to about 1½ inches. The trapezius should be shaped from the back as far as that can be done, the narrowed buttress still being retained.

Fig. 52. The head is approaching completion, although the neck is still nonexistent. Work on the shoulders with point and claw tools has been begun.

All this work must be done with the tools used in the same order as they were used in carving the head: first the point, then claw tools, finer claw tools, gouges, chisels, and finally (although not at this stage), rifflers or emery.

Final Stages

The last stages of the work include not only the final shaping and finishing of the contours of face and shoulders, but also the removal of the two buttresses or supports to the neck and the cutting free of the bust from the larger block. The final work on the head can hardly be described as if it were only a technical process, because no description can do more than suggest things to study and common faults to be avoided, if possible. The student's capacity of perception is not a fixed quantity, and everything is dependent on that. I have described several common errors which students are likely to make, and it will be noted that I have assumed that sculpture has some relation to the forms of nature; but even if this assumption is denied, the technique of chiseling remains the same as I have described. A stylism based on simplification and enlargement of certain parts may give a monumental quality to the forms. I am certain that sculpture does not consist in the reduplication of the forms of nature in another material; but I have deliberately assumed that in making a portrait bust it is well, and necessary, to aim at achieving a recognizable likeness; although the almost infinite subtlety of nature cannot and should not be attempted in the translation into marble or stone, yet there remains the indisputable fact that the distinguishing features in which personal character reside must be the basic elements in the representation if a likeness is to be achieved. Any student who has studied a cast from a head, either a life or a death mask, must feel that such forms are not sculpture, and that copying them into stone or marble cannot make sculpture.

I have warned students of the danger of seeking too early to record the minutiae of form; yet now, in the later stages, I would suggest that a student use all the powers of perception and observation, and all the capacity for expression, of which he is capable, to record in a harmonious whole those minute and subtle details in which character, spirit, and even soul, may be visible to an understanding mind. It is relatively easy to make a formula for a face or a figure, but if a formula is what the student is seeking let it at least be an expressive formula and one based on a synthesis of the forms rather than on the simple device of leaving out all the difficult detail. How far the student will pursue the search for significant and characteristic detail is his or her own decision, and I have no wish to be didactic; I will not try to give him any rule that will tell him when to stop the work. It may be carried to an extreme degree of finish and yet be an indifferent achievement or it may be expressively carved with a minimum of detail and no high degree of finish and still be successful and even distinguished. No finish could improve the roughly carved bust of Brutus by Michelangelo. It is already charged with nobility and spirit; but an exquisitely finished bust by Houdon or Flaxman, or a good Roman bust, is also a work of art, and the meticulous finish and surface detail does not necessarily lead to any loss of sculptural style. *Style* should be sought with all one's powers, but work should not be *in a style*.

On the strictly technical side, the bust now requires that the slender neck be shaped with great care; first of all because of the fragility of marble, and also because the neck is the means by which the head, instead of being left as an isolated group of features, is made to take its place as a part of the body. It is well to remember that the column of the neck is short and is not set vertically but on an angle. (See fig. 53, *a*.) The back of the shoulders or, more technically, the trapezius muscle, comes up the back of the neck, about to a level with the chin,

A CHILD'S HEAD

narrows, and continues up to its point of attachment to the skull. (Some anatomical study is useful to a sculptor.)

A child's neck is almost always wider across the front than from front to back; it is not circular. (See fig. 53, *b*.) Although in the stone the supports, back and front, make it difficult to shape a neck, it must nevertheless be attempted while they are still in place. The best way is to keep narrowing the but-

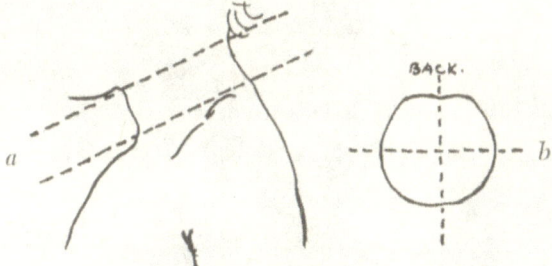

Fig. 53. *a*. Axis of neck. *b*. Section of neck.

tresses and at the same time shaping the contours of the neck so that they are in register across the buttress. There can be no hard hammering, yet the marble must be chipped away. On the chest and back the buttresses can be narrowed so as almost to allow the shoulders to be shaped and finished. The aim is to leave the very minimum of work to be done after the buttresses are removed.

To remove these, use a hack saw and cut a series of grooves across the marble, not more than ¼ inch deep and about the same distance apart. With a narrow chisel, clear between the saw cuts; then make more saw cuts and continue clearing between them. Work on both front and back buttresses, keeping both at nearly the same stage. Each successive reduction toward the neck makes it more fragile, but as the buttresses are removed the unity of the work appears and it becomes possible to see it as a completed whole, the head merging into the neck and the neck into the shoulders and bust. The final delicate

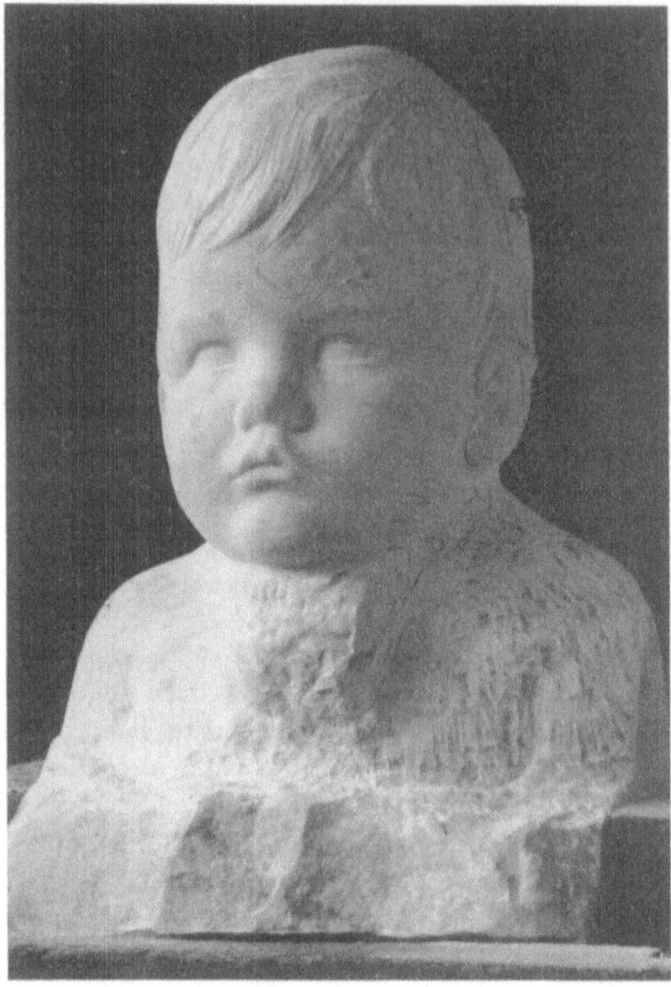

Fig. 54. The shoulders are being shaped with chisels; the neck is beginning to appear. Both front and back buttresses have been narrowed.

shaping of the neck, with its creases and muscular structure, can be accomplished by the use of curved rifflers, preferably 10 or 12 inches long (straight rasps are of little use). With these a good deal of delicate modeling can be done, and strips of emery cloth (blue back), first No. 2½ or 2, and then finer, are

A CHILD'S HEAD

useful in obtaining a final surface. But remember that emery abrasives and rasping tend to lose modeling rather than to achieve it. Chisels and gouges are the tools to use, and rifflers are mainly used to remove ridges and awkward traces of chiseling and, when required, to get a smooth surface. Curved and rat-tailed rifflers are useful for shaping and smoothing the neck, as using them does not jar the neck, with consequent risk of breakage. After the neck is reduced to its final slender shape it is not wise to risk any working with hammer and chisel on the head or hair, although there is less risk in working on the shoulders and bust. Caution is born of experience, and few persons who have worked much in marble or hard stone have not had bitter and costly (even if salutary) experiences with fractures and breakages. I have not myself used the many electrical abrasive devices which are now available and which would undoubtedly lessen the risk of breakage. Electrical or pneumatically controlled chiseling would almost certainly increase it. I would have been glad to use an emery saw to cut the bust off the block, but none was available, so I had to saw it off by hand, using 12-inch hacksaw blades—two blades in the saw at a time. This makes a wider saw cut and is perhaps a little less likely to saw unevenly. I sawed both from the back and from the front; it was almost a day's work to get through the five inches or so, and it blunted three pairs of saw blades. But the cut was fairly smooth, and in order to get the final surface so that the bust would stand on a base I rubbed the bust on a flat board covered with a large sheet of the coarsest garnet paper. This very quickly gave it a good level surface and the bust was finished.

To sum up, I would suggest: In the rough shaping work, aim at character and try neither to see, nor to express, detail; seek the generic rather than the individual features, and then try to isolate in your mind the distinctive characteristics which express the personality of the model or sitter (who isn't just

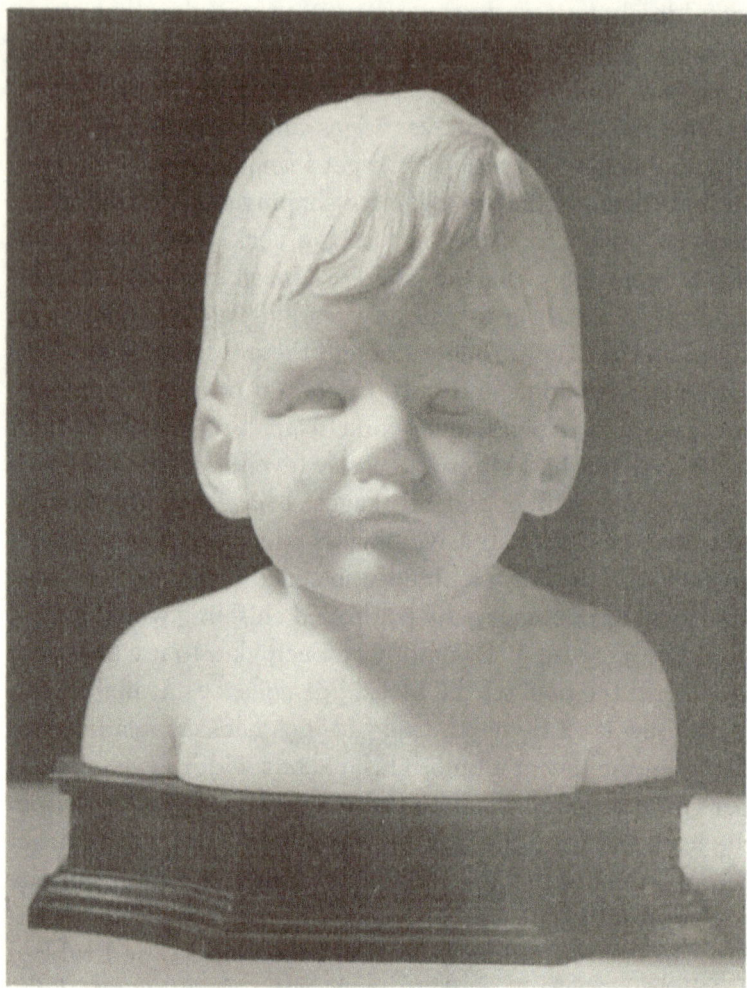

Fig. 55. The finished bust on a walnut base. The whole proportion and design have been changed by cutting the bust horizontally at the armpits, thus contrasting the vertical oval of the head with the horizontal oval of the bust. (Total height, about 11 inches.)

sitting, but must be studied), and try to show these. Once this is achieved for the actual features and contours of the face, carry the work to such a degree of verisimilitude and finish as is consistent with the material, the sense of style, and your artistic conscience. A stage may well come when one feels that to carry the work further is to risk the loss of the likeness or of the stylism. The decision has to be made; but do not too readily stop the search for the subtle and final beauties of surface, and, above all, do not be seduced by a love of effects into leaving unhewn and rough masses of stone or marble because these make an effective and spectacular contrast with such parts as are highly finished. Such contrasts are highly artificial and should not be exploited. They arise temporarily as one works but should not be made permanent. Seek form rather than effects.

A work of art may be slight and insignificant in scale, but it should be conceived as a whole and carried throughout to the same degree of completion.

CHAPTER 8

Carving a Draped Figure in Limestone

I must repeat that the method here described is entirely personal, and may indeed seem peculiarly so; but I believe it to be much nearer to the method and practice of the medieval carvers than the modern method of making a clay model, casting that in plaster, and then copying the plaster in stone. But the test of any method of working is the result, and a student would do well to try different methods of working, and from them to develop a technique congenial to his own temperament and outlook. Too great boldness in tackling problems of carving without having thought out the forms, or without having worked them out in drawings or a model, may well lead to trouble and disappointment; but, conversely, too much reliance on drawing or modeling may lead to timidity and diffidence in carving, and may perhaps even react on character, for carving direct is a process requiring clear concepts and a certain amount of audacity of handling.

I have chosen here a common medieval subject, and in pose and disposition of draperies the figure is reminiscent of the work of that period. The subject is a universal one, and every sculptor is likely, sooner or later, to be called on to represent maternity in some form. In my own practice, the method described is exactly the same whether the subject is a draped figure, as here, or a nude or seminude figure for, say, a garden statue.

It will be seen that the preliminary sketch, reproduced in figure 58 (p. 108), is not very detailed and does little more than show the action of the two figures and the main lines of the disposition of the drapery. There is an indication in blue pencil of the figure beneath the drapery, and the sketch is done on the usual basic division of height into about 7½ heads. But a sketch like this gives little help when one begins to translate it into a third dimension. It will be noted, for instance, that nothing can be seen of the entire left shoulder and arm of the Madonna, and the right arm is seen in perspective. This makes it impossible to take measurements from it; hence I find it wise always to make a diagram of the figure, with indications of the main joints in the skeleton. (Such diagrams are admirably shown in the last chapter of Thomson's *Anatomy for Art Students*.[1]) From this, shown in figure 60 (p. 114), the measurements can be taken; for instance, the upper arm is about 1½ heads long, the forearm about 1 head, and the hand about ¾ of a head. The length of the legs can be measured from the trochanter to the kneecap and thence to the ankles. Similarly, the width of the shoulders, although not seen from the front, can be measured from behind, and will be found to be nearly 2 heads. All this may seem somewhat mechanical, and a rigid adherence to a scale may not be always necessary, but, as approximate sizes, I find them useful and corroborative. I have added in the diagram of the female figure a similar diagram of the child's figure, which also gives the relative sizes. This is most essential, as a proportion has to be observed between the two figures. It will be seen that the child's figure is a little less than half the adult one, and that the child's head is a little less than one-fourth its height. This is for a child of between one and two years. (See fig. 60.)

I have already suggested that in getting a block of stone for

---

[1] Arthur Thomson, *A Handbook of Anatomy for Art Students* (5th ed.; New York: Macmillan, 1930).

A DRAPED FIGURE 105

a statue some (but not too much) margin should be allowed. For the present 3-foot figure of a mother and child I allowed a margin of nearly an inch in width and depth, which is ample.

Stage I

With these drawings before one, the first rough shaping can be done, using first of all the pitcher, then the big claw tool; the essential thing to aim at is to approximate the disposition of the main masses and to get rid of the squareness of the block. It will be seen that the block of stone is held between two blocks of wood nailed to the bench and is also supported behind by a stout wooden strut nailed to the bench and to a beam above. These fastenings are less necessary when one is doing the final work, but in the early stages, when hard hammering has to be done, it is essential that the block be held steady. The preliminary shaping is simple and aims at no more than removing the corners of the stone and getting a suggestion of the action of the figure and a rough indication of where the child will be. No approximation to the contours of a figure is possible as long as there are square sides to the block. For the convenience of fixing, it is well to keep the base of the block square and heavy as long as is possible.

Stage II

Figure 57 shows the beginning of the shaping of the features, and it will be seen that the head is defined at a very early stage. This is because the head is the basic unit of proportion, and therefore to define its size and action is essential. It is well to set a pair of calipers to the full size of the head, which may be had from the nude drawing, allowing a little extra for the drapery and headdress; also to set a pair of compasses to the half head (chin to eyes). The bulk of stone, being heavy, and the proportions and scale of the figure hardly defined, the size of the head always appears incredibly small; but it is necessary

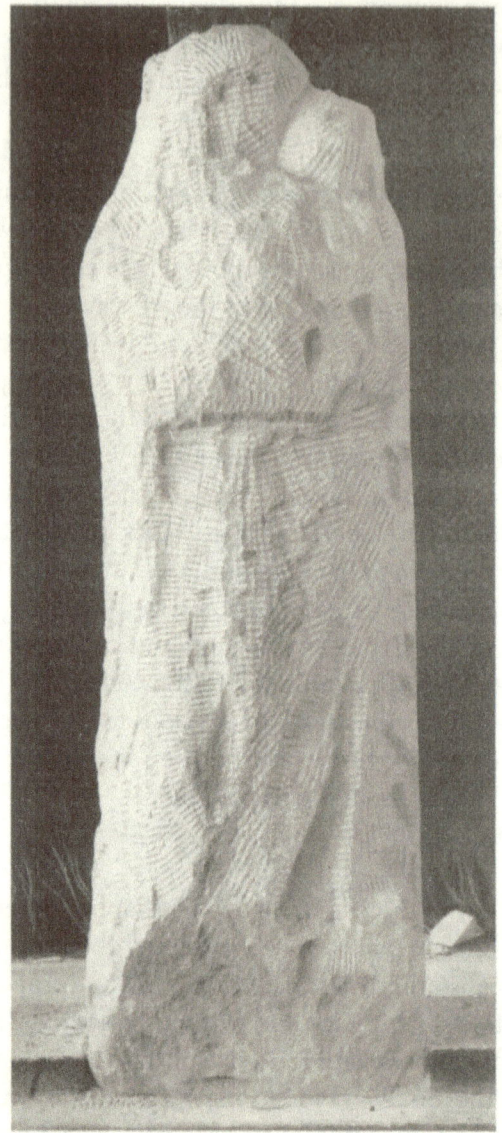

Fig. 56. The first rough shaping of the block consists mainly in getting rid of the square sides, using only the pitcher and a large claw tool.

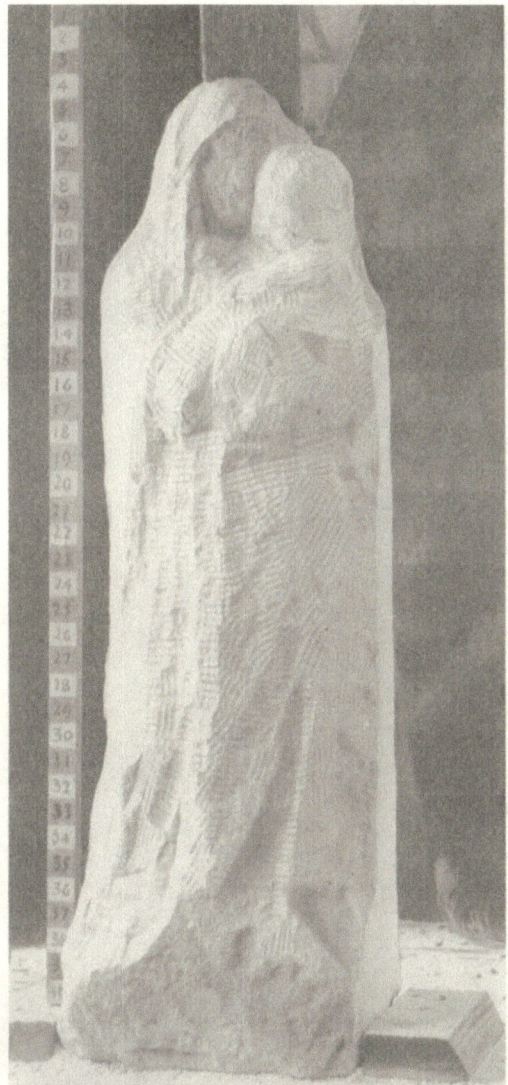

Fig. 57. The forms of the figures are being defined, and the position of the arms and the child suggested. The scale is indicated by the size of the heads.

Fig. 58. The shaping of the long, radiating lines of drapery with the bolster has been begun. The drawing is not quite full size, but measurements are all taken from the nude scale drawing (fig. 60).

A DRAPED FIGURE 109

to hold to one's scale, allowing only a small margin (perhaps, on the scale of this head of about 4½ inches, ¼ inch is sufficient). One must be careful not to get the eyes too high; it is impossible to add later to the head, but easy to remove something from the top if the eyes are too low. Shape an oval for the face, eyes to chin, with the merest indication of the projection of the nose and shape of mouth. The action of the head must be indicated at this early stage, and where two heads are close together, as here, it is necessary to shape both heads at the same time. The scale of the child's head can be obtained from the nude diagram (in a child's head, the middle of the head is not at the level of the eyes). It will be seen that the pose of the child in the carving is more upright than in the preliminary sketch, as thus a rather hunched-up appearance is avoided and a greater simplicity is given to the pose. Action and movement natural and appropriate in a picture may not be suitable in sculpture, and the student must remember that compactness of composition is necessary. The child's arms must not project forward without support.

As the figure is gradually shaped, it will be found that the head, which seemed so small, fits into the scale of the figure. I repeat, from the earlier chapter on the marble head, that one has to be careful that forms or features are kept in proportion, and that one can allow only a narrow margin of enlargement. The forms should be kept a fraction large, but not too much, or the scale becomes altered. If the head is too large, instinctively one shapes the shoulders to the scale of the head, and then discovers that the stone isn't tall enough for this enlarged figure. This is the reason for the nude diagram, and I would never work on a figure, whether in a simple or complicated action, without first making such a guide. Figure 58 shows the beginnings of the disposition of the drapery, shaped roughly with a large chisel (which may be either toothed or plain), and already the position of the child and the composition of the

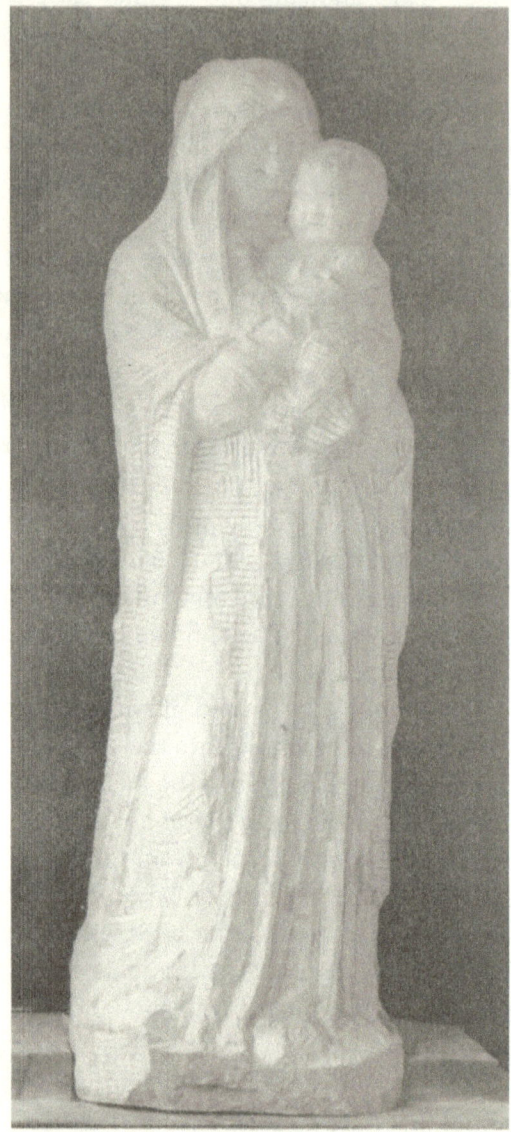

Fig. 59. The curved action of the figure is becoming evident with the gradual diminution of its bulk. The composition of the lines of drapery is being indicated.

A DRAPED FIGURE

upper part of the figure are indicated. That upper third of the block contains certainly two-thirds of the work on the statue. In the next stage it is worked out a little more fully, but even at this stage an effort must be made to shape the mother's arms, the child's body, and the two heads into a unity of lines and contours.

Stage III

It is now time to concentrate on the composition of the upper part. The first essential is to get the two heads to about their right size and grouped harmoniously. This is done with smaller tools, still mainly claw tools, ranging from ½ inch to 1 inch wide, some bullnosed chisels, and a few gouges. I would use chiefly fine-toothed chisels, say about ¾ inch wide and with perhaps six or eight teeth.

With the face of the Madonna roughly shaped and in scale, work the drapery over the shoulders, the width of the shoulders being about 2 heads, which includes drapery. Large calipers, opening to 14 or 15 inches, are useful in taking measurements. One should follow down from the shoulders toward the elbows, and then down the forearms to the hands. Here again, the diagram should be consulted for size of hands, length of forearm, and so on. The hands, when first indicated, always seem as if they must be too small, but the drawing should nevertheless be adhered to. A hand from the wrist to the tip of the middle finger is about ¾ of a head, and on an average the width of a hand is about half its length.

Again, if measurements seem mechanical, I repeat that these are approximations and only to be used as such, although they are often useful. The central line which in this figure passes through the head to the inner side of the left ankle, can be checked in the carving by using a plumb line. This is always a useful aid in preserving the stance of the figure. The deep fold of drapery which passes over the right arm and down the right thigh should be indicated, and care must be taken that the

112   STONE AND MARBLE CARVING

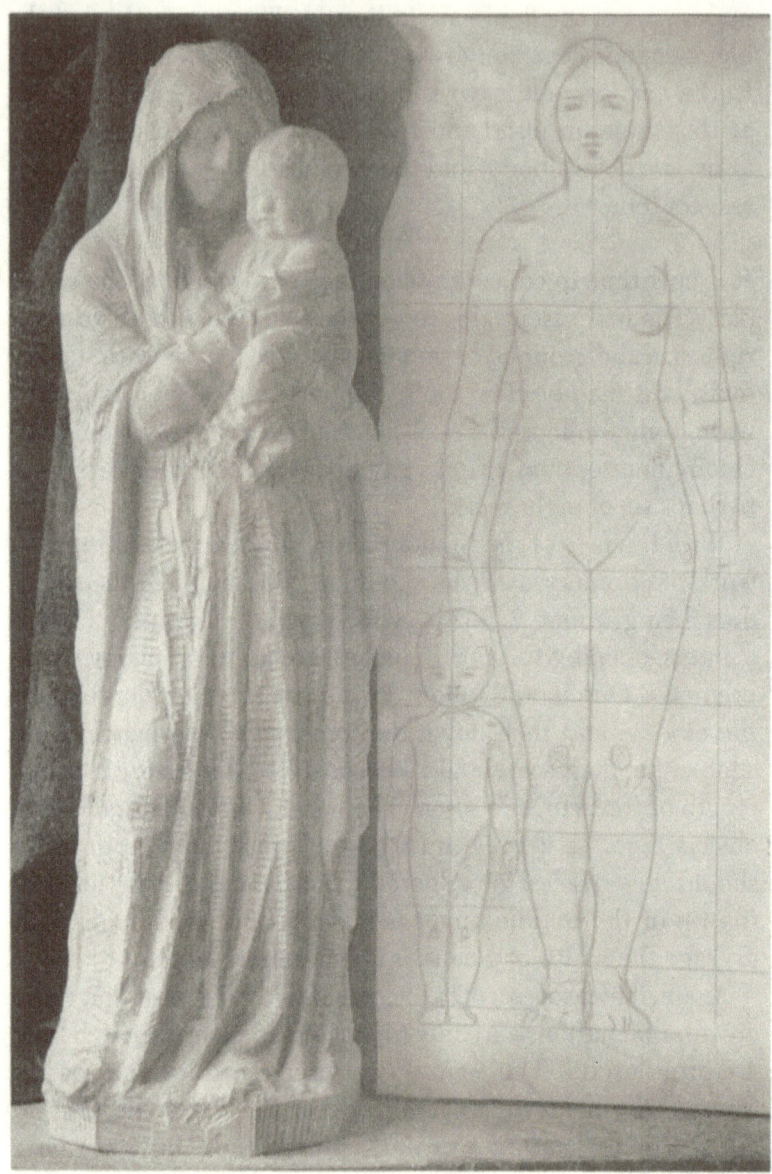

Fig. 60. Progress toward complete realization of action of both figures is being made. The draperies are more exactly defined and disposed. The scale drawing of the figures is used constantly to check measurements.

stone does not fracture here. Particular care should be taken, if there are shells or fossils in the stone, and undercutting should be avoided until much later, when all the dispositions of the drapery are fixed. The child's drapery is slight and of a very simple shape, but the Madonna's drapery is more elaborate and its lines and deep folds require some concentrated effort. There are sculptors who would design this by draping a lay figure or a plaster statue and copying the resultant folds realistically. I would prefer that a student should study casts and photographs of good medieval work if real examples are not within reach. No student of sculpture can neglect these lovely figures.

It can be said that from the twelfth to the early part of the sixteenth century there is an almost steady progression toward more and more complete realism. In the twelfth-century figures at Chartres, or the early thirteenth-century work at Wells, realism is consciously, or unconsciously, kept at a distance, whereas in the last phases of fifteenth-century work, and in the work of the early sixteenth century—as in the great ambulatory screen at Chartres,—the draperies are often almost illusively real. Sometimes even the textures of different stuffs are indicated and velvet is distinguished from linen or woolen garments. But I do not think it is possible to understand the best medieval sculptured drapery if one considers it as drapery or clothing, as these late Gothic sculptors did, or as lines forming a design, as did the early Gothic carvers; it should be conceived and designed as moldings, and a study of the sections of drapery is far more important than its realistic representation. This was pointed out many years ago, by, I think, Professor Lethaby. I am convinced that it is the right way to study, and the right approach in one's own work. I am certain that I never understood the true beauty of medieval sculpture until I studied it with an eye to sections of moldings. It will be seen from figure 60 that the deep folds of drapery are not,

Fig. 61. The draperies have been worked into deep, molded sections with gouges and rifflers; the Madonna's face has been given expression, and the action of the Child is clearly defined.

A DRAPED FIGURE 115

as in wood carvings, shaped with deep gouges, run in vertical grooves, but are worked with chisels or claw tools used from side to side. Too great regularity in width of folds should be avoided; there should be variety, some parallelism and some radiation in the folds, and variation in the depths.

The feet should be so indicated that the drapery may break over them. The average width of a foot is about ½ of a head, and its length is about one-sixth to one-seventh the height of the figure.

Final Stages

The final stages develop gradually from the earlier ones. Folds of drapery have to be deepened and curves modified. It is well to note that draperies fall, not in actual curves, but in faintly angular shapes; also, that where the fold takes a new direction is where it is thinnest. But these touches of realism should not make one forget that the aim is to achieve a series of interesting and expressive sections.

In finishing the arms it is well to work from the hands upward, first of all establishing the scale. This applies to both the mother and the child. The left arm and hand, on which the child is carried, are always more difficult, as they tend to be partly hidden. It will be seen that the child's hands are both attached—in fact there are no sharp projections anywhere, for these are likely to break, either in the process of carving or afterward. The compactness forced on one by the necessity for strength is an essential part of designing for stone sculpture.

The deep recesses of drapery can be finished and deepened by the use of large rat-tailed rifflers, and some of the finishing of the round edges of drapery or contours can be done with coarse blue-back emery. The degree of finish to aim at will depend on many things; the position in which the finished figure is to be placed, its lighting, and height from the ground, as well as the nature of the stone from which it is carved. If the

Fig. 62. The completed statue.

figure is to be placed in a niche, its back need not be so much detailed; and the child's neck may be supported at the back by some unhewn stone, which will not be seen from the front. It is well to avoid even the appearance of fragility.

In working the deep recesses around the neck it is well to use very thin and very sharp tools, and occasionally drilling may be useful, especially if the stone is at all hard. The edges of rifflers may be used as saws, and this saves risk from hammering; but it is with the chisels and gouges that one gets the best contours. As rifflers and abrasives tend to minimize one's modeling, they should be used chiefly for the finishing, rather than for the shaping, stages. A saw and a large coarse rasp may be used for finishing the base block and also for the back.

With regard to the faces, one should not try to finish the features until the action is defined, nor (as was discussed in the chapter on the marble head) to undercut until the very last stages. It is necessary to get the scale of the head fixed in an early stage, but the final detail of features and expression should be left until all the rest of the figure is at least shaped. One should seek for expressiveness and a true sculptural style, but the "stoniness" of the stone need not be obtrusive.

The theory of preserving the quality and beauty of stone by neglecting to shape it to expressive contours has been carried to some lengths; but there remains to us the example of innumerable medieval sculptures on every church or cathedral built during the centuries of Gothic work, and these preserve and indeed dignify the material, stone, while at the same time they are filled with emotional power and beauty. Let these be our examples, and, while refusing to copy or imitate them, let us seek to initiate forms as true and moving as they, for what hampers the artist today is not the examples and traditions of the past, but the conventions and theories of the present.

Index

Abrasives, 99
Alabaster, 27
Angle of holding tools, 51–52
Angle of incised letters, 44

Banker, mason's, 14, 73
Base-bedded stones, 22
Bench, height of, 73
Bolster, 29–30
Box-fastening to hold block, 72
Breakages, 21, 99
Bronze tools, 7
Buttresses (supports to head), 95

Caen stone, 23
Callousing of stone surfaces, 22
Carborundum, 7, 35
Carrara marble, 20, 69
Carver, medieval names for, 2–3
"Chase," 69–70
Claw tools, 36–37, 86
Cloth, representation of, 112
Clothing, sculptor's, 38–39
Compactness in sculpture, 109
Compass, used in measurement, 85

Death mask, 95
Drapery, 112–113
Drawing, sculptor's, 14, 59–60, 104
Drill, 92–93
"Dummy," 32–33

Ear, position of, 82–84
Emery cloth, 36, 98
Emery wheel, 35
Eye, 77, 91–92

Face-bedded stone, 22
Facial angle, 77
"Feathers and wedges," 70

Finish, degree of, 101
Fixing stone for carving, 71–73

Gill, Eric, carving technique of, 46
Gothic foliage, 51; sections of, 57
Gothic lettering, 49
Gouges, 32, 58
Granite, 27
Gritstones, 24

Hacksaw, 97
Hair, treatment of: in relief, 66; in head, 86–90
Hammers, 33–34
Head, in figure, 105–107

Indiana limestone, 20–23

Lettering: books on, 41; incised, 41–47; raised, 47–50
Limestones, 19–20

Marble, 25–26, 69 ff.
Margin allowed in size of stone, 31, 105
Measurements: head, 74–75; figure, 104
Measuring devices, 81–82
Medial line, drawn in face, 82–83
Mirror, to check asymmetry, 82
Modeling, distinction between carving and, 15–16, 86

Neck, 97

Oölitic limestones, 19–21

Perceptive faculties, 87
Pitcher, 31, 60–61
"Plucking" of stone, 22

Plumb line, 111
Point, 32, 51–52
Pointing instrument, 16–17
Portrait: relief, 59 ff.; head, 69ff.
Proportions: of figure, 104, 113; of child, 109

Quadrature, 8–10

Reduction scale, 75
Rifflers, 38, 98–99
Roman lettering, 41 ff.

Sandblasting, 28
Sandstone, 24

Saws, 29–30
"Scabbling," 32
Serifs, in lettering, 44–45
Shells in stone, 21
Sicilian marble, 26
Squares, to check division of face, 81
Stones: list of, 20; weight of, 28
Style, 96

Tape measure, 82
Tempering of tools, 35
Tools, 29 ff.; sharpening, 35–37
Trapezius muscle, 93

Undercutting, 78, 82, 83, 85

www.ingramcontent.com/pod-product-compliance
Lightning Source LLC
Chambersburg PA
CBHW021714230426
43668CB00008B/826